HOOSIER CENTURY

100 years of photographs from
The Indianapolis Star and
The Indianapolis News

Compiled and edited by Charlie Nye and Joe Young
Text by Charlie Nye

THE INDIANAPOLIS STAR

COVER: Melinda Gibson of Lancaster, N.Y., rolled through Boone County as part of her group's 100-mile ride. The Wheelmen, the common name for the 3,000-member national organization of antique-bicycle riders, were holding their four-day meet in Indianapolis in July 1998. (Photo by Paul Sancya)

TITLE PAGE: Indianapolis brothers Matthew (front) and Raymond Schnorr were all smiles in anticipation of the 1959 Indianapolis 500 as they sat in a car built by their 18-year-old brother, William. (Photo by William Palmer)

BACK COVER: Photographers covering the Adlai Stevenson campaign in Indianapolis in October 1952 had a unique angle from which to shoot. They were (clockwise from top left): Dean Timmerman, *The Indianapolis Times*; William Palmer, *The Indianapolis News*; Maurice Burnett, *The Indianapolis Star*; Ralph DeWeese, Bass Photo; and Ruth Chin, independent. (Photo by Bob Lavelle)

Library of Congress Catalog Card Number: 99-67185
Hoosier Century: 100 years of photographs from *The Indianapolis Star* and *The Indianapolis News*
ISBN 1-58261-237-4

Published 1999 by Sports Publishing Inc.
www.SportsPublishingInc.com
Printed in the United States

DESIGN: Channon Seifert, Charlie Nye, Scott Thien
CAPTION WRITING AND COPY EDITING: Roxanne Morgan, Lawrence S. Connor
PRODUCTION: Alex Waddell, Jeff Atteberry, Steve Curd, Tom Lund, Larry Dailey, Tony McGlan, Kevin Anderson, and Ed Saipetch

Dedication

This book is dedicated to the memory of publisher Eugene S. Pulliam (1914-1999), who began his newspaper career in Lebanon as a paperboy for *The Indianapolis News*. Pulliam (above) and his father, Eugene C. Pulliam, who bought *The Indianapolis Star* in 1944 and *The News* in 1948, had a vision for newspapers that transcended the dissemination of information. They wanted readers to welcome *The Star* and *The News* into their homes like family. Generations of readers stand as a testament to how successfully that goal was met. Not only were readers seen as an extension of the Pulliam family, the papers' employees were as well. The newpapers, and the city, can attribute much of their greatness to the leadership and humanitarianism of this great man.

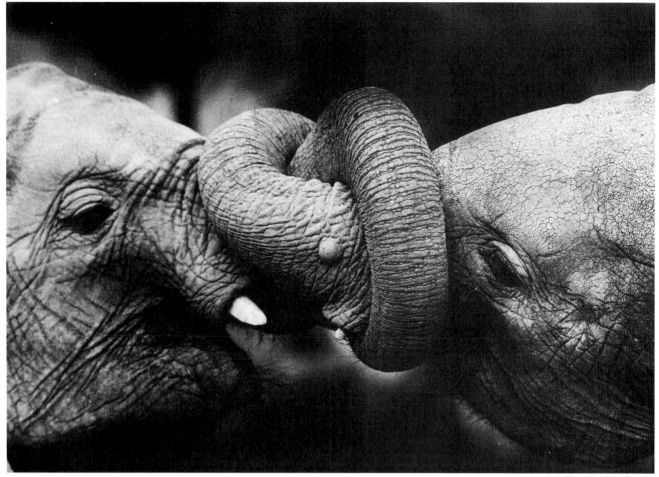

Photo by Rob Goebel

These baby African elephants appear quite wrapped up in each other as they await their turn in the spotlight. The performers entertained audiences in Indianapolis during a visit by the Carson & Barnes 5-Ring Wild Animal Circus on May 28, 1985.

Acknowledgments

This project would not have been possible without the concerted efforts of many current and former employees of *The Indianapolis Star* and *The Indianapolis News.* Their assistance in researching photos has been invaluable. We would like to thank the following for their hard work in making this book come to fruition: Sandy Fitzgerald, Charlesetta Means, Rasheed Fazle, Rebecca Cline, Barbara Hoffman, Terry Wall, Laura Kehoe and Kathy Knapp; Frank Caperton, Nancy Comiskey, Ted Daniels, Steve Greenberg, Lisa Masariu, Sharon Martin, Janet Baker, Dale Duncan, Kimberly Parker, Tim O'Keeffe, Cori Faklaris, Shirley Roberts, Dave Hill, Greg Fisher, Mike Fender, Alan Petersime, Karen Ducey, Mpozi Tolbert, and Kim Travis; retired photographers Frank Fisse, Bob Doeppers, George Tilford, Ed Lacey Jr., Larry George, Jim Young, Jim Ramsey and John Starkey; reporters Nelson Price and Kelly Kendall for their help with text; reporters/former reporters Diane Frederick, Harley R. Bierce, Thomas R. Keating, Jeff Swiatek, Wendi C. Thomas, Andrea Neal and Mark Rochester for excerpts from published news accounts; special contributors Chuck Scott, Chip Maury, Lori Borgman-Nye and Linda Kelso; Stephen J. Fletcher and Susan Sutton of the Indiana Historical Society; and Joe Bannon Jr. and Terry Hayden of Sports Publishing Inc.

Table of Contents

It didn't take long for pediatric neurologist Dr. Bradford Hale to draw a crowd at the Methodist Hospital Children's Pavilion in September 1989. The physician, a father of five, had played in a variety of bands, ranging from traditional jazz to bluegrass to the Indianapolis Municipal Band.

Introduction

Photographs tell stories of everyday life with the universal language that is emotion. Great photographs evoke an emotional response from a viewer — a chuckle, empathy, tranquility, delight, anger or surprise.

Without the element of surprise, life becomes dull and flavorless. The great challenge for a newspaper photographer is to capture the variety of life — defining moments as well as quiet and uneventful times — in images and to present it to readers in a new and refreshing way each day. Woven into the pages of a daily newspaper, these images produce a grand portrait of a people and the land they inhabit.

In this book, we set out to assemble a vast array of images from *The Indianapolis Star* and *The Indianapolis News* that represents the most striking and significant photographs from the past 100 years. Some images are riveting — Parnelli Jones leaping from his burning race car; a hostage with a sawed-off shotgun pointed at his head. Offsetting such startling images are others, likewise as engaging but of a serene nature — the sea of faces in a children's choir, or baby African elephants playfully knotting trunks backstage at a circus.

There are photographs celebrating both the ordinary and the extraordinary: 94-year-old Isaac Drew, possibly Indiana's oldest practicing farmer, climbing over an iron gate on his way to a grain bin. There are slice-of-life images from every decade, images of the famous and the infamous and everyday people doing everyday things: Dan Quayle jubilantly raising his fist while campaigning with his presidential running mate, George Bush, in 1988; and, from another era, a milkman setting bottles of milk on a doorstep.

Some images reflect contemporary life at the turn of the new century, while others remind us of the past. Posing for an *Indianapolis News* photographer, legendary Notre Dame football coach Knute Rockne projects the image of strength and success. A panoramic Cirkut camera view taken in 1907 shows President Theodore Roosevelt addressing about 50,000 people at the courthouse in Indianapolis.

With few exceptions, all of these pictures were taken by *Star* or *News* staff photographers who, day after day and year after year, have come face to face with Hoosiers in all walks of life, documenting their good times and bad. Several of the images were taken by stringers or commercial photographers commissioned by the newspapers.

Selecting the finest and most significant pictures taken for the papers over the course of this century has been a journey of discovery — or, more precisely, rediscovery — as long-forgotten images were pulled from the archives.

What is not in those archives is a painful reminder that *The Star* and *The News* weren't always as inclusive in their coverage of this racially diverse community as we have tried to be in recent years.

Editing the selections for this 208-page book was a tough task, and hundreds of fine pictures, showing historical events or notable Hoosiers, were left out. We have selected pictures that not only represent the variety of life in Indiana in the 1900s, but are outstanding examples of photojournalism. We believe the contemporary pictures (from the past 25 years) are images that will stand the test of time.

As the 20th century draws to a close, so does a chapter in the history of photojournalism in Indianapolis. With the closing in October 1999 of *The Indianapolis News* after 130 years, this photographic treasury takes on additional value as the greatest collection of *Indianapolis News* pictures within the covers of one book.

— Charlie Nye, Assistant Managing Editor for Photo and Graphics

Charles F. Bretzman (1866-1934), who took the Theodore Roosevelt photo for *The Indianapolis News*, was born in Hanover, Germany, and came to the United States in 1885. He got started in the photography business in 1895 with a studio atop the Fletcher Trust Building, and specialized in portraits. He also was the first official photographer for the Indianapolis 500. His son, Noble (1909-1986), took over the business after Bretzman's death.

| CHAPTER 1 |

Behind the Lenses

O ne of the most remarkable news pictures ever published in an Indianapolis newspaper was taken May 30, 1907, in the infancy of the 20th century. *The Indianapolis News* commissioned Indianapolis commercial photographer Charles Bretzman to photograph President Theodore Roosevelt addressing a crowd of 40,000 to 50,000 people outside the county courthouse. Using a rotating panoramic Cirkut camera, Bretzman made several lengthy exposures as the massive crowd stood motionless, intently listening to the president.

The amazing camera produced a negative 8 feet 7 inches long. A 6-foot portion of that negative was reproduced the next afternoon in *The News*, spanning two inside pages, or 16 columns. The original of the photograph was displayed in *The News'* window for two days. Bretzman headed to the darkroom to fill orders for reprints coming in from newspapers and magazines. Deluged with requests, the paper made smaller reproductions available for sale to the public.

Two days after the photo was taken, an article headlined "Remarkable Photo of a Remarkable Crowd" said the president's visit caused such a commotion "that never in the history of kodaking in Indianapolis were there so many wrecked machines turned in as on yesterday. And never so many films and plates to be developed." The article went on to say the "photographic supply men" surmised that the reason for so many broken cameras — or machines, as they called them — was that the president "moves so rapidly that the amateurs would rush after him and, with their eyes fastened on the focusing glass, would run into trolley poles and other obstacles."

At the time, *The News*, billing itself as The Great Hoosier Daily, had only one photographer, Paul Shideler, who was hired as an office boy in 1903 at the age of 15. It wasn't long before Shideler started taking pictures for the paper. News photography was relatively new to Indianapolis in those days. To get to assignments, the enthusiastic young photographer had to walk, run, bicycle or take a trolley

car, all the while lugging along a bulky camera, tripod and other items weighing about 50 pounds.

The load got easier for Shideler about 10 years later when the newspaper hired a second photographer, and even more so when photographers began to travel to assignments in Model T roadsters. "The Big League had arrived," said Shideler, reflecting on that exciting development years later.

The early days of the 20th century generated some exciting and tense moments for Shideler and his contemporaries. Flash powder, for instance, was used to illuminate subjects before the introduction of flashbulbs or electronic strobes. Scooped onto a hand-held metal trough and ignited, the powder could be quite dangerous. It created a bright burst of light, enabling photographers to record images on glass plates, which had very low sensitivity to light.

Shideler depended on flash powder to provide adequate light indoors for his subjects. Each fall, he accompanied the Republican Club of Indianapolis on its weekend retreat at the Palmer House in Chicago. Shideler and the politicos made the trip aboard the Riley, a famous train run between Cincinnati and Chicago. His assignment was to get a picture of the gathering in the old hotel ballroom.

Using flash powder, Shideler had only one chance to make a picture of the group because the flash powder sent out a big cloud of smoke, fogging the air. As he described it, he would set the camera securely on the tripod, then pull out the flash powder and ignite it. He'd never get another shot off: The place quickly filled with smoke. As Shideler high-tailed it for the door, people behind him bellowed, "Where's the damn photographer?"

Shideler made another trip with the Republican Club after the advent of flashbulbs. On the Riley, all the way up to Chicago, he told everyone what a great step forward bulbs were: No more smoke and no more noise, and they could shoot as many pictures as they wanted. No problem. Subsequently, he got the politicians all lined up for the pictures. Still talking about how there would be no smoke and how he could take lots of pictures, he fired off the first shot. The bulb burst, sounding like a howitzer going off, and ground glass blew all over everybody.

A reflector he had rigged from the old flash-powder gun was too flexible and had leaned forward onto the bulb. The instant the bulb

Above is the first half of a 360-degree Cirkut camera photograph of an appearance by President Theodore Roosevelt on May 30, 1907. That day, as many as 50,000 people gathered in Downtown Indianapolis for a major policy address by the 26th president. *The Indianapolis News*, which commissioned the photo from commercial photographer Charles Bretzman, built a special platform from which to take it. The view includes East Washington Street (left) and North Delaware Street. The three buildings (above, from left) are Tomlinson Hall, City Market and the Marion County Courthouse, where Roosevelt and other dignitaries appeared on a platform on the west steps. The photo continues on the next two pages.

Indianapolis News photo

Paul Shideler (above) started at *The Indianapolis News* as an office boy in 1903 and became its first photographer. Shideler (1888-1962), shown with his 4x5 Speed Graphic and flash-powder gun, retired as chief photographer in 1956. *The Indianapolis Star's* first photographer, Joseph Craven (below, with his 4x5 Speed Graphic), arrived in 1922. Craven (1887-1963) retired as chief photographer in 1953.

Indianapolis Star photo

went off, the heat went to the reflector and then popped back out again. The incident was good for a big laugh. Shideler finally figured out the problem and was able to use bulbs without them exploding.

* * *

Shideler's industrious 53-year career spanned the years from the first Indianapolis 500-Mile Race in 1911 to the advent of smaller cameras, which were just coming into vogue when he retired in 1956 as *The News'* chief photographer.

Shideler's counterpart at *The Star* was Joseph E. Craven, who, along with Shideler, had covered every Indianapolis 500 from the beginning, until his retirement in 1953. Craven's father was a portrait photographer in Marion in the 1890s, a profession that required exposing printing paper to the sun because the emulsion was not very light-sensitive.

When Craven came to Indianapolis in 1909, he started working for Charles Bretzman in his commercial department, then went to *The Indianapolis Sun* and opened the first photo department for that newspaper in 1911. He left *The Sun* and opened his own studio, but newspapers were too much in his blood; he eventually was hired by *The Star*, where he worked for 31 years, beginning in 1922.

Nearly 100 photographers have worked for either *The Star* or *The News* over the years. Photographs appeared in *The News* since before the turn of the 20th century, and in *The Star* since its debut on June 6, 1903. *The News* was the city's oldest newspaper, established Dec. 7, 1869, and published six days a week, until ceasing publication after its Oct. 1, 1999, final edition.

Star and *News* photographers have logged millions of miles on assignment throughout the "Crossroads of America," creating a rich visual documentary of this quaint Midwestern state, birthplace of such diverse personalities as David Letterman, former Vice President Dan Quayle, President Benjamin Harrison and singer/songwriter/producer Kenneth "Babyface" Edmonds.

Competing staffs of *News* and *Star* photographers covered Indianapolis for 92 years, until the photography staffs of the two Pulliam papers were merged in 1995. Photographers set out with a singular purpose: to record the people, places and events of their time. In directing their cameras toward raging fires, thrilling sports events, campaigning politicians, hard times and good times, photographers

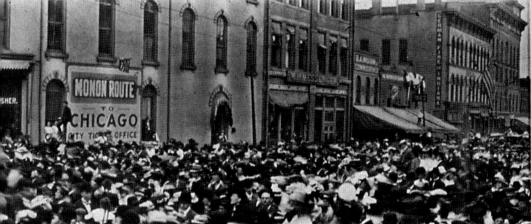

have documented the unfolding story of life in Indiana from birth to death. The ever-present cameras relentlessly clicked away, day after day, year after year, decade after decade.

While some photographs in this book received accolades and won awards on state or national levels, many had minimal exposure beyond their publication. After the film was processed, printed, then filed away, the pictures faded from memory over time. The fleeting moment passed; a new day delivered new deadlines, challenges, pictorial subjects and new roads for photographers to travel. Most were acknowledged with a tiny credit line under their photographs, but newspaper photographs early in the century went mostly uncredited.

Great pictures don't necessarily require great subjects. Many spectacular photographs are made of commonplace events and ordinary people in mundane settings. What sets these images apart, elevating them to a higher plane, is the photographer's art of seeing, resourcefulness or persistence.

The pictures speak for themselves; yet many interesting stories lie behind the pictures, tales that are just as interesting as the final photographic results. While times have changed and the tools the photographers use have improved, the photojournalists' resolve to make the best pictures possible remains fundamental to their job.

* * *

Halloween night in Indianapolis in 1963 was unfolding much like any other. Youngsters dressed as Cinderella, goblins and tattered hobos had their bags filled with candy. But that night would forever be marked by one of the worst disasters in the city's history, because inside the Indiana State Fairgrounds Coliseum, a real horror of grotesque proportions wreaked havoc on an unsuspecting audience.

The Holiday on Ice performance was nearing the finale when leaking gas from a propane tank in a concession area under the seats was ignited by an electric popcorn warmer. The powerful explosion hurled dozens of people onto the ice, up to 60 feet away. *News* photographer Joe Young was one of the staffers who scrambled to get to the site of the tragic accident, which killed 74 people and injured about 400 others. Positioning himself high in the stands, Young framed the overall scene in a Veriwide camera and made one of the most memorable photographs ever taken in Indianapolis — dozens of bodies covered with blankets on the ice, where the coroner set up a

The second half of commercial photographer Charles Bretzman's 360-degree Cirkut photo shows East Washington Street and South Delaware Street. All of the buildings in both sides of the photo are gone, except for City Market (see page 9); the courthouse was replaced by the City-County Building. A 6-foot section of the 8-foot-7-inch negative was reproduced by *The Indianapolis News* in 16 columns across two pages on May 31, 1907, quite a feat at the time. *The News* displayed a large original print in its window and released the rights to Bretzman, who filled many orders for reprints. The public was able to purchase smaller reproductions.

Ready for action in 1963 with a 35 mm Leica IIIG, *Indianapolis News* photographer Joe Young (above) took a picture that year that became etched in a city's memory: bodies laid out on the ice at the State Fairgrounds Coliseum after a gas explosion that killed 74. Photographer Jim Young (below, and no relation to Joe) covered the Tony Kiritsis hostage ordeal for *The News* in 1977, a job that required a lot of hustle and two stops to buy more film.

temporary morgue.

Covering this type of horrendous event is, unfortunately, one aspect of a photojournalist's job. Neither pleasant nor welcome, such assignments are sometimes unavoidable. More characteristic of a newspaper photographer's day is the photographing of the mundane and ordinary: buildings under construction or summer festivals. Pictures of frolicking children and beautiful scenes offset the disturbing situations a newspaper photographer has to shoot. Still, adrenaline-rush breaking-news situations will always be a part of the job.

When *Indianapolis News* photographer Jim Young walked into the office on Feb. 8, 1977, 70-year-old photographer Horace Ketring was putting his galoshes on. "They've got a hostage situation and they want me to go, but do you want to go?" Young was game, so he grabbed a camera with an 85 mm lens on it and two half-rolls of film. In those days, Young said, if you took only five or six pictures, you were supposed to cut those out of the camera and use the other end of the roll for another assignment.

Young hustled down to the scene, a bank one block down the street. "There's a lot of cops standing outside on the other side of the street, and a TV photographer was there, too," said Young.

"Then the door across the street flies open and all these guys come runnin' out. This guy in a business shirt comes out. And I'm looking at him, and they turn, and when they turn, there's a man with a shotgun at this guy's head," said Young.

It was the beginning of a three-day ordeal that seemed destined for a tragic ending. Upset over a business deal with Meridian Mortgage Co., Tony Kiritsis pulled a gun on Richard Hall, the company's president, as he arrived for work.

Outside the building, Kiritsis searched in vain for his car in a parking garage. When he couldn't find it, he marched Hall down the street. Young, following the action, ran into a former reporter and told him to call the paper and get someone to meet him with some long lenses.

Young was really nervous at this point: "I was down to my last frame — I had already shot both of my half-rolls. When we went by Stationers, I went in with about a dollar and a half in my pocket. I bought one roll of film with all the money I had."

Young wasn't the only photographer having a bad day. Jim Schweiker, the United Press International photographer, heard about the incident and took off running toward the scene. It was very cold, and there was a lot of ice on the ground. He hit the middle of Ohio Street, slipped on the ice and broke every camera he had.

Kiritsis continued to lead Hall down the sidewalk, then turned onto Washington Street, police all around him and all the traffic stopped. Kiritsis was cursing and screaming. Before long, Young was out of film again, so he ran into the H. Lieber Photo Store, saying, "I need film. Give me film! Give me film!"

The clerk said, "Well, how much you want?"

"Give me a handful. Give me a handful."

She put out about six or seven rolls on the counter and Young ran toward the door, telling her, "Charge them to *The News*."

"You'll come back and sign for those, won't you?" she asked. Young kept going. The clerk called the photo lab to verify that Young worked for *The News*, but by that time he was a block away.

Another *News* photographer, Gary Moore, showed up carrying long lenses. Police were trying to stop traffic, and Kiritsis was going down the middle of the street. A policeman had left his car parked in the intersection, sideways, with the door open and the motor running. Kiritsis got to the car, backed in, pulled Hall in, and they drove to Kiritsis' apartment complex.

They holed up there until, on the third day, Kiritsis stepped out of his apartment to conduct an impromptu news conference, still wired to Hall. Young was on the scene to make a dramatic picture. After Kiritsis had his say, he released Hall unharmed and gave himself up.

Star chief photographer James Ramsey put his neck on the line to get pictures during the newspaper's expose of illegal gambling in the 1960s. He knew he would get caught, but he had to take a chance.

"We shut down the gambling operations in Terre Haute, shut down the whorehouses in Terre Haute," said Ramsey, who made many trips around the state to shoot pictures of gambling establishments. "Then came that fateful night in East Chicago, when reporter Ernie Wilkinson and I got caught," Ramsey reminisces. "This would have been a tremendous picture. This was a poker game, and there were some very well-known Chicago political figures sitting around the poker table. The first pot, as near as I could calculate from listening to it, was $32,000. And I think they were anteing something like $2,000 or $3,000.

"I had a Leica with a 21 mm super-angulon lens strapped under my shirt, and all that I had to do was to open that shirt and hit the button. And when I opened the shirt, some guy up front said, 'That guy's taking a picture!' We were in a long, narrow room. There's a chain across there, and up in front of the chain was a table. And it was probably about 12, maybe 15 feet from the chain."

With his hands sweeping from left to right, Ramsey continues his story: "Back here was a crowd, I mean a crowd of spectators, just watching that poker game. And I sneaked up, wove my way through, so I could get right up next to the chain. Well, immediately, when the guy said, 'Pictures!' the rest of that room emptied. Fast. I mean quick. And only Ernie and I were left standing.

"We made for the door, but we didn't get there, because we were up front. Everybody else was gone by the time we got there; somebody slammed the door, so we were left inside. I didn't want them screwing up the camera, so after an hour or so of discussion, I took the film out for them. In the meantime, though, I was standing back from the table and I had a pool cue in my hand." Ramsey and Wilkinson were permitted to leave, but it gave them a scare they would never forget.

Bob Doeppers, chief photographer of *The News* from the '60s to the mid-'80s, had a harrowing encounter of his own, with a similar ending in that he escaped unscathed.

Photo by Jeff Atteberry

James C. Ramsey (above) was the fourth chief photographer of *The Indianapolis Star*, which he joined in 1952. He was a pioneer in the use of color photographs in *The Star*, overcoming opposition from management at all levels, and pushed for use of The Associated Press wire photo transmitter to cover news and sports throughout the state. Stranded Downtown during the Blizzard of 1978, Ramsey captured on film the deserted city center. He retired in 1985.

Bob Doeppers (above) worked for *The Indianapolis News* from 1952 to 1987 and retired as its third chief photographer. In that role, the man everyone around the paper called Dep worked "the early shift," being first in the lab each morning. His on-the-job adventures included a hurried exit through a plate-glass window. Correspondent photographer Jerry Mouser (below) was injured in a tornado while on assignment for *The News*.

Doeppers was sent out to photograph the scene of a weekend break-in at a tavern in the late '50s or early '60s. "The owner of this well-known bar and restaurant was in there early Monday morning," said Doeppers. "I talked to him for about 15 minutes and suddenly —and I don't know what was said, or what led up to it — he took a swing at me.

"And of course, having a Speed Graphic in my hand, well, I was able to get that up quick enough to protect me. I just kept backing away from him. I wanted to get out of there in a hurry and I just backed right through the plate-glass window in front. I hit it in such a way, though, that all the glass fell away from me."

Three photographers for *The Star* were not as lucky when they covered a Ku Klux Klan rally on the steps of the Statehouse in Downtown Indianapolis on Oct. 16, 1993. Photographers Patrick Schneider, Kelly Wilkinson and intern Joe Stefanchik were among at least seven people injured during skirmishes that erupted after the rally by 35 Klan participants. The event was attended by an estimated 1,000 people, including hundreds of anti-Klan demonstrators, hundreds of police and scores of Klan sympathizers.

Barricades kept onlookers about 100 feet from the Klan, but the photographers turned into targets of crowd violence that broke out as the rally ended. Stefanchik was hit in the back of the head by a young black man with a wooden 2-by-4 plank. "He just came up and hit me and started laughing. He knocked me real hard. I got real dizzy," said Stefanchik, who, like the other photographers, is white.

Schneider believed the photographers were ambushed for their cameras. "When they couldn't get them from me, they whipped me into the ground," he said. Holding onto his cameras, he was jumped by three men. He wrenched his knee when he was hurled to the ground.

Wilkinson was photographing an Associated Press photographer being punched when someone threw her to the ground. "They were kicking my head," said Wilkinson. "They just kept kicking me, and I yelled, 'Please stop!' " Wilkinson, who had one of her cameras and a radio stolen, was treated and released from the hospital, as were the other photographers.

On assignment in Fairland, Jerry Mouser, a correspondent photographer for *The News*, escaped serious injury when he was caught up in a tornado on March 10, 1986. Mouser was sitting at a country-style dinner with 78-year-old dairy farmer Raphael Reuter and his family when hail began pummeling the two-story wood frame farmhouse. They went to the back porch to look out at the sky and saw a tornado coming their way. "As I turned to go into the kitchen, it blew me to the floor," said Mouser. "I tried to crawl into the house, but I couldn't move. I felt like I was pinned in the vacuum." He managed to get inside, where "the walls shook and the roof started to give way. The house was moving, and the floor shook. Windows exploded like a bomb going off. My mouth and eyes were full of dust. Glass and dishes and pots and pans were flying through the fog."

When the 30 seconds of terror subsided, Mouser and four others emerged shaken. The house had been shifted 2 feet off its foundation. Within 15 minutes, with rain still falling, the area was filled with neighbors and State Police. "Even before the storm stopped," Mouser said, "35 or 40 farmers were at his place helping them out. One guy came down on horseback to see if they needed help." Mouser's face was bleeding, but he thanked God that he lived to tell about it. That afternoon, tornadoes and thunderstorms that plowed through the state's midsection left two people dead, dozens injured and hundreds of homes and businesses damaged or destroyed.

Disasters from the sky come in different forms. The first edition of the Oct. 20, 1987, *Indianapolis News* was just about to go to press at 9:15 a.m. when a dispatch came across the newsroom police scanner that an Air Force fighter jet had just crashed into the Ramada Inn near Indianapolis International Airport. Initial reports were sketchy — 25 people were feared dead from the crash of the jet, which lost power while returning from a training mission.

News chief photographer Mike Fender jumped in his car and headed at breakneck speed toward the tall plume of black smoke up ahead. When he arrived at the scene, Fender saw the tail of the burning jet jutting out of the front entrance of the 220-room Ramada, with 130 hotel guests and employees inside.

The pilot had ejected, parachuting to safety as his stalled aircraft spun on its descent. After clipping the roof of a nearby bank branch, the jet plunged through the hotel lobby and exploded in a ball of fire, killing 10 people. Fender quickly shot several rolls of film, then drove back to the paper to process and print.

A dramatic six-column photo ran across the front page of the Home Edition of *The News*, with three more pictures inside. Rushing his pictures out on deadline, Fender then returned to the scene to take more pictures, alongside other *News* staff photographers and those for *The Star*, which didn't go to press until the next morning.

Photographers for the two newspapers have experienced an amiable, although competitive, working relationship on assignments. Wanting to outshoot a competitor, a photographer occasionally looked on the travails experienced by the other photographer with a degree of amusement.

Retired *Star* photographer Frank Fisse recalled one such incident that took place many years ago at old Victory Field. The Indianapolis Indians were playing a day game, and Bob Lavelle, chief photographer of *The News*, was up on the roof to get a different angle. Fisse looked over and saw Lavelle all excited. Lavelle had been shooting with a Graflex camera, designed in such a way that a photographer had to look down a long chute to compose a picture. The camera was sitting beside Lavelle when the sun shone down the chute, hitting the mirror. It magnified the sunlight, setting the camera on fire. "The camera was smokin' away," said Fisse, chuckling.

Even funnier was the time that Fisse saw five flashbulbs go off in *News* staffer Frank Salzarulo's pocket. "He flicked one bulb in there," said Fisse, "and it went off, setting off all the others — light was coming out from his pocket! Those things were dangerous! You'd get a burn on you if you weren't careful."

Another story of disaster averted has to do with Shideler. While photographing an Armistice Day parade in Indianapolis early in the century, he scooped too much powder onto the flash-powder gun. When it was fired, the gun broke, sending it soaring 50 feet into the air. It came back down, hitting Shideler in the head. Fortunately, the photographer was wearing a derby and was uninjured.

The use of artificial lighting early in the century could make a photographer's job quite an adventure. Bob Hoover of *The News* told about an anxious moment he had while photographing a burrowing bootlegger during Prohibition. This fellow had set up elaborate head-quarters in a sod-covered underground room, which had access through a manhole.

The police learned of the hideaway, and Hoover, doubling as re-porter and photographer, went on the subsequent raid with his old camera and a supply of flash powder for illumination. "Well, I set off the flash with a big 'whoooommmmm' and the roof caved in," Hoover related. "That was one slightly contaminated batch of hootch that wasn't worth confiscating."

Dale Schofner of *The Star* once covered a concert at Tech High School, which was notorious for its bad lighting. "Nobody would ever get a picture in there, because the lighting wasn't very good," said Fisse. In order to illuminate the spacious area, Schofner went to great effort to set up seven lights with slave units, devices that fired off the flashbulbs when the initial flash was fired. "He had the slaves down the side and had just finished setting up the last one. He was ready to go," Fisse explained. "He got out front and looked into the camera for one last check, when some kid from the school news-paper walked in. Then BANG! All Schofner's lights went off." The student had taken a picture with his small camera, setting off all the flashbulbs. "Schofner had to go replace all the bulbs to take his shot. The kid sure got a great picture!" said Fisse.

Under adverse circumstances — be it darkness, access or limited time — photographers resort to old-fashioned ingenuity to make good pictures. One of the most trying feats has been coverage of the Indianapolis 500, which Indianapolis newspaper photographers have photographed since the very first one on May 30, 1911. *The News'* Shideler was among a crowd of 100,000 at that first race, won by Ray Harroun in a 6-hour, 42-minute, 8-second endurance test.

Drivers and photographers alike have constantly battled time. Years ago, when the race was run on traditional Memorial Day, *The News*, an afternoon daily, put out a special Extra edition. All the pages except for Page 1 would be on the press and ready to go near the end of the race. As soon as the winner could be determined, the front page was finalized and the winner proclaimed in a big, bold headline accompanied by his picture. The press would roll and a helicopter would fly fresh-off-the-press copies of the paper to the track at the edge of town. While still in Victory Circle, the winner would be handed a copy of the paper. Receiving accolades from the crowd, the driver would wave around the newspaper with a screaming headline declaring him the winner.

Lloyd's of London, which provided the helicopter insurance, determined what would happen if the helicopter ever crashed — hundreds of people would have been killed and injured. "The company raised the insurance premiums," Ramsey said. "I think they wanted about $1.4 million to insure that helicopter for that one day. That's when we stopped using it."

To get a special angle for their pictures of the race in 1958, Young and fellow *News* photographer Dean Timmerman worked out a deal with the owner of a two-man lift. The photographers climbed into the bucket placed on Turn 3 and gleefully watched as they were raised in the air above their green-eyed cohorts on the ground. Despite that superior vantage point, Young was dissatisfied with where the track placed them. "Nothing ever happens on the third turn!" he said. But as it turned out, the biggest race car pileup in Speedway history occurred on the first lap that year — right in front of them in the third turn. One driver was killed.

For the next three years, *The News* took a lift out to the track until giving it up in 1961. As former chief photographer Doeppers recalls, everybody and his brother tried to do it, and the Speedway put the kibosh on it.

The Speedway constructed a photographers' stand at the end of pit row, a wooden structure holding dozens of people. But in 1971, pace car driver Eldon Palmer, a local auto dealer, lost control after turning into the pits at the start of the race and plowed into the stand, injuring 22. Sixty photographers representing newspapers and magazines from around the world tumbled out, some on top of the pace car,

Photo by Joe Young

Four-time Indianapolis 500 winner A.J. Foyt (above, with wife Lucy) could read all about it right away after winning his second race in 1964. Until the 500 was moved to Sunday in 1970, copies of *The Indianapolis News Extra* were rushed by helicopter to the track after the race. In 1958 and 1959, *The News* rented a Strato-Tower to get a better angle on the 500; photographer Bob Doeppers used it in Turn 1 in 1959 (left).

Photo courtesy Indianapolis Motor Speedway

Local auto dealer Eldon Palmer, driving the Dodge pace car for the 1971 Indianapolis 500, slid out of control in the pit area at the start of the race (top photo). The car then struck the photographers' stand at the end of pit row, throwing about 60 people to the ground (lower photo). *Indianapolis Star* stringer Louis J. Schumacher shot the top picture from the stand; he fell from its first tier and landed in the pace car, which also carried astronaut John Glenn, sportscaster Chris Schenkel and Speedway owner Tony Hulman. The accident left 22 people injured, including 10 who were taken to Methodist Hospital.

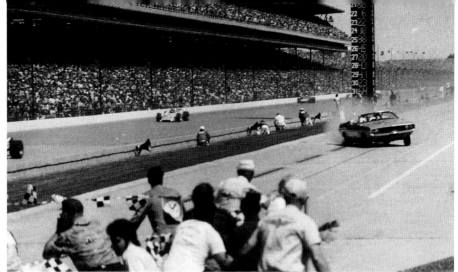

Photo by Louis J. Schumacher

Indianapolis Star photo

some on the ground and some on top of each other.

After swerving back and forth, knocking down observers, the pace car slammed into the stand at a speed estimated at 40 to 70 mph. Astronaut John Glenn was in the front seat with Palmer; ABC television sportscaster Chris Schenkel and Speedway owner Tony Hulman were in the back seat of the convertible. Glenn said he was looking at the track and didn't know what happened until the impact.

You never know quite what to expect while covering racing at the Speedway, in large part because of the interesting personalities out at the race track. Photographer Larry George said, "I've never forgotten A.J. Foyt. The first time he came to town from Texas and started racing, we wanted to get a picture of him for the newspaper. We were at some reception of some kind. And he wanted to know how much my newspaper was going to pay him to have his picture in the newspaper. And I said to him, 'We don't work it that way here. You know, this is a public news thing that we're doing and nobody gets paid. This is not a model agency!' "

Fisse tells a story of a man at the track who'd do anything to get in a picture. "They have a crash car at the 500," said Fisse, "and every time there's a crash, you get in the car and go out to the scene. Well, there was some guy who was a friend of Tony Hulman (owner of the track). He was an insurance man. Every time there was a crash, he'd run and get in the crash car and go to the scene. He'd get behind the injured driver and he'd be in every picture.

"Well, the managing editor called me in and said, 'Who is this jerk?'

"And I said, 'Well, he's a friend of Hulman's.' He said, 'Well, how come he's in all the pictures? I don't want that guy in another picture!'

"Well, three days later, a guy hit the wall and he spun up there. So I'm trying to watch the injured driver when they take him out of the car, and I'm trying to keep an eye on the guy so he doesn't get in the picture, so I don't catch hell about it. So I print the picture. In the best one, there he is. He's standing right there, helping them get him out of the car. You know, he's not a medical guy, or anything else. So, boy, I don't know what to do. I went to the managing editor and said, 'Well, he did it to me again!' He said, 'Take it back there and have Sweeney (an artist) paint him out.'

"So I went back there and told Gil Sweeney . . . I said, 'Can you make this guy look like a mechanic or change his face or something?' So I pick up the paper the next day and there's a tree there, right behind the car — it's got bark and leaves. A perfect damn tree. Boy, the best-looking tree you ever saw. There's no guy there, but this damn tree is there.

"So I go out to the track the next day and someone said, 'Hey, Superintendent (Clarence) Cagle is looking for you.' I say, 'Well yeah, I bet he is.' So Cagle says, 'Frank, I've had two guys with chain saws and I had another crew out.'

"The Speedway had received 35 calls that morning, calling them reckless bastards, saying, 'You're going to kill a driver. You know, that guy just missed a tree. It was right there by the car.'

"I said to Cagle, 'Yeah, I know, we painted this guy out.' So then he called Bob Early, the managing editor, and he got it from him."

Because of poor photo reproduction on letterpress, touching up photographs so they would print better was a common practice. But often, editors got carried away in what they insisted on being touched up. Some of the things that photographers were prohibited from showing included bellybuttons, men's nipples, tongues hanging out, women's cleavage and midriffs. If pictures were turned in with this forbidden content, the artist's brush would make them acceptable for publication in a family newspaper.

"We used to shoot the fashions for Ayres and Block's and Wasson's before they hired their own people," said Doeppers, "and we'd shoot whatever they sent out for us to photograph. If we had a low-cut swimsuit, or a low-cut blouse, we went ahead and shot them. The assistant managing editor at the time would just have the artist paint in a smaller cleavage. There were a number of people who called up and complained about the artists doing too much work on their clothing, because whoever designed the item wanted it to look the way it was supposed to."

Some editors were not deterred. When fashion designers started making two-piece swimsuits instead of one, an artist was told to turn a two-piece suit in a picture into a one-piece to cover the belly.

Photo by Harold L. Jorio

Indianapolis Star photographer Frank Fisse (above) kept in touch with the newpaper's city desk via two-way radio in 1956, after the equipment was installed in the cars of photographers for both *The Star* and *The Indianapolis News.* With him in the Ford wagon was his 4x5 Speed Graphic. Fisse worked for *The Star* from 1946 until retiring in 1989.

Photo by Ed Lacey Jr.

The Indianapolis Star's **Ed Lacey Jr. (above) was assigned to photograph a snake found in a case of bananas by a fruit wholesaler. Finding no one willing to hold the snake, Lacey put the camera on a tripod and, using a self-timer, photographed himself gripping the reptile. While the story made the paper, the picture did not; editors thought it would be too disturbing to readers early in the morning.**

The "breakfast table" factor came into play when potentially offensive pictures were considered for publication. Photographer Ed Lacey Jr. went out to photograph a bushmaster snake that had come out of a case of bananas at an area fruit wholesaler. "The guy was bitten, but he was OK," said Lacey. "We couldn't use the picture, though, because of showing a snake that early in the morning." Lacey, lacking a volunteer, held up the snake himself for a camera on a tripod, and his picture went out on The Associated Press wire and ran in papers all over the country. Not in Indianapolis, though.

Today, photographers don't worry about two-piece swimsuits, tongues or bellybuttons offending readers. They take great care to be sensitive to what might be offensive. Bodies of fatally injured people, for instance, unless covered by blankets, are generally not published. Editors place great emphasis on the need to maintain credibility with readers. Photos are not touched up to alter or sanitize content as they were decades ago. The newspaper has established strict policies against photo manipulation, especially since today's sophisticated computer software makes it relatively easy to move parts of a scene around or to fabricate a photograph altogether, as supermarket tabloids do.

Photojournalism does not shy away from serious topics, even photos that surely would have been considered offensive 30 years ago. Several pictures of this nature were published in the fall of 1993 as part of an project localizing a hot national issue — health care.

The nation was in the midst of a debate on the government's role in providing quality care. Spending on health care in the United States had more than tripled in the previous dozen years.

To give readers a personal look at the quality of care, *The Indianapolis News* dispatched 32 photographers throughout Indianapolis and nearby communities to photograph dozens of health care facilities, medical schools, physicians, patients and businesses on the front line of health care during one 24-hour period, on Oct. 15, 1993.

During the course of the day, the bulk of the newspaper's photo staff, supplemented by free-lance photographers and photojournalism students from several universities, shot more than 200 rolls of film illustrating the scope of the quest for good medical care. The result was an eight-page section published one week later, illustrated with 59 pictures. Photographs included the birth of a child, a portrait of a 36-year-old man who had contracted AIDS through contaminated needles, and a man on a stretcher with blood streaming down his face.

Times have changed in other ways. Back when Shideler and Ray Myers were *The News'* only two photographers in the late teens, they would get an opportunity about once a week to shoot something having any chance of getting into the paper. Shortly before he retired, Shideler explained to Doeppers that there was room for only a couple of pictures a week. Because everything was shot on glass plates, with an extremely slow emulsion speed, the newspaper mostly used woodcuts during the first years he worked. Woodcuts are carefully drawn simulations of photographs copied onto a smooth block, on which a craftsman cuts away all the surface area except the lines to be printed. (By 1910, hand engraving started to become obsolete in U.S. newspapers, as the halftone process became widely accepted.)

Today, with the use of digital cameras and instantaneous transmission of pictures from remote locations, photographs can be taken just minutes from deadline. When Indianapolis played host to the NCAA Final Four basketball tournament on March 31, 1997, *The Star* and *The News* set up three portable computers on the ground floor of the RCA Dome. During the national championship game between Arizona and Kentucky, more than 80 pictures were transmitted back to the newspaper, many of them just minutes after being shot.

Of the 22 pictures used in the special section the next morning, at least a dozen were from digital cameras, including a five-column-wide celebration picture on the front page, which was shot at the end of overtime, nearly a quarter past midnight. The presses rolled close to schedule, about 1 a.m. Without digital cameras, *The Star* could not have published as many pictures from late in the game.

* * *

This collective treasury of *The Star* and *The News* photographers' work stands as a testament to the power of the photograph and to the insight of the photographers. This book provides an opportunity to sit back and reflect on the past 100 years, the people of Indiana and the events that shaped their lives. No one knows for sure what the next century will bring, but one thing is certain: Whatever happens, photographers will be there to record the events and create images to share with present and future generations.

Long lenses enable sports photographers to get a close-up look at faraway action. In July 1988, the long lenses were out in force as the national media covered the U.S. Olympic Track and Field Trials at the stadium at IUPUI (below left). Nearly four decades earlier, in 1950, *The Indianapolis Star* bought a rapid-sequence camera (below right), which was used for the first time by chief photographer Dale Schofner at an IU-Ohio State football game. The K-24 aerial sequence camera weighed 50 pounds and made 4x5 exposures on a long roll of film.

Photo by Frank Espich

Indianapolis Star photo

CHAPTER 2

Photo by Jim Young

Holding a shotgun to mortgage company executive Richard Hall, Tony Kiritsis herded him along a Downtown street on Feb. 8, 1977, before commandeering a police car and taking Hall to Kiritsis' Westside apartment. Sixty-three hours later, Kiritsis emerged from his home, held a news conference, freed his hostage and surrendered. Kiritsis said Hall's firm cheated him. At right, firemen Larry Tucker, Lt. Phil Reuter and Lt. Steve Cook (from left) rescued Pauline Williamson from Downtown's Barton Annex on Feb. 10, 1989.

Eyewitness

News is the primary fodder for photojournalism: raging fires, accidents, heated political campaigns and organized efforts to right societal wrongs. Time is of the essence for visual journalists rushing to a news event; minutes can make the difference between a great picture or returning to the office empty-handed.

News photography is a competitive business. Photographers compete not only against time, but against their own abilities. They strive to see beyond the obvious and create images that capture the essence of an event.

To make memorable images, the photographer has to be in the right spot. He has to find the right angle and the best lighting and anticipate the moment of peak action.

Alert to every possibility that could unfold before the camera, a photographer engages his mind like a chess master who constantly asks himself, "What will happen next?" and "Where should I move?"

By making the right choices, a photographer can create images that engage readers both intellectually and emotionally.

Indianapolis firefighters (facing page) held onto 32-year-old Clarence Eddie Abbott on Feb. 2, 1977, to keep him from plunging 150 feet off the Indiana World War Memorial. After 20 minutes, Lt. Don Graston and Pvt. Dan Gammon were able to pull him up.

Four pups made it out of a burning home, soggy but safe, in the arms of Indianapolis firefighter Joe Woolsey on Nov. 7, 1970. A fellow firefighter retrieved three other pups. The dogs' mom, Sissy, escaped under her own power from the blaze at 915 N. Highland Ave.

Photo by William Palmer

A monkey up a tree brought police and firefighters to the Southwestside on Sept. 22, 1964. The animal ignored bananas, then leaped down and away as a firefighter headed up. It finally was nabbed by Patrolmen John Palmer (left) and Richard Dorsey.

Indianapolis Star photo

25

Indianapolis News photo

Former Indianapolis Mayor Samuel "Lew" Shank (above) hit the streets on a sled one winter around 1914. Shank's first term as mayor, 1910-13, ended when he resigned during labor troubles. He then went on the vaudeville circuit, performing a monologue about being mayor. Shank was elected to a second four-year term in 1922. He died in 1927. Not even a sled could be seen on Ohio Street (right) on Jan. 26, 1978. Indianapolis' worst blizzard had dumped more than 15 inches of snow on top of 5 already on the ground.

Photo by James C. Ramsey

Heavy rains flooded the 1800 block of Centennial Street on Indianapolis' Westside in the early 1960s, separating this youngster from her tricycle. The picture earned *The Indianapolis News'* George Tilford a second-place finish in The Associated Press' national photography contest.

Photo by George Tilford

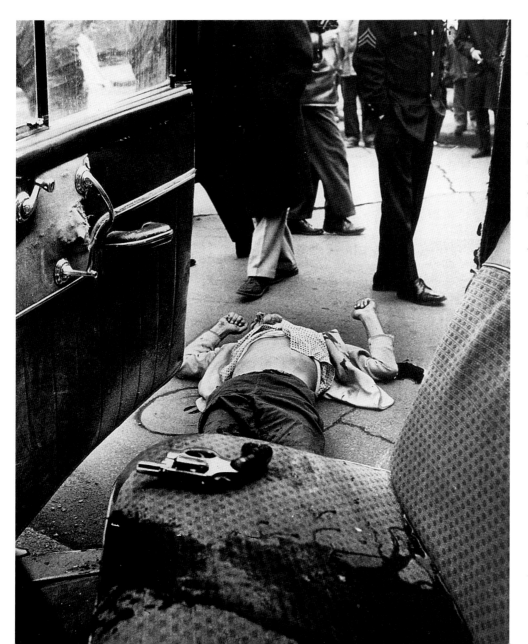

Almon Meredith, who was accused of a killing at a trailer court and the wounding of an Indianapolis policeman, was hit by police bullets on Jan. 12, 1963, at Market and Pine streets in Indianapolis (left). A gun allegedly used in the crimes lay on the seat of a car that had been driven by Meredith.

Photo by James Ramsey

Indianapolis defense workers went wild at the news that Germany had agreed to an armistice on Nov. 11, 1918, bringing an end to the horror and destruction of World War I. This photo, shot in the first block of Kentucky Avenue, looks south from near Washington Street. "The Great War," which began in July 1914, took the lives of nearly 10 million troops. The United States lost 116,516, including nearly 3,400 Hoosiers. Wounded Americans totaled 234,428. Among the United States' fellow Allies in the war were future enemies Serbia, Cuba and Japan.

Photo by Paul Shideler

An Indiana-Kentucky company of candidates for the Army Officers' Reserve Corps drilled with bayonets (right) at Fort Benjamin Harrison on May 22, 1917, during World War I. The post was established in Indianapolis in 1903 and was closed in 1995, with part of the property being converted into a state park.

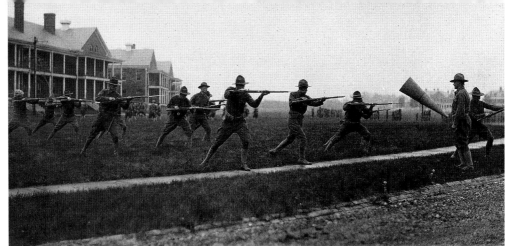

Photo by Ray Myers

Mr. and Mrs. George V. Bedell of Indianapolis (above), uncle and aunt of Lt. Gen. Walter Bedell Smith, who accepted Germany's surrender in World War II on May 7, 1945, listened intently to the news in their Marlowe Avenue home on May 8, V-E Day, when the surrender was announced. On May 16, ticker tape, confetti and colored streamers filled the air (right) as the vanguard of a "Peace Parade" moved south on Pennsylvania Street. Thousands thronged Downtown streets and sidewalks to celebrate the end of the war.

Indianapolis Star photos

Thousands of Italians captured in World War II were interned at Camp Atterbury in southern Johnson County. The War Department, after blacking out recognizable faces of Italians working at the camp on June 13, 1943, approved the photo for publication. That summer, the prisoners built a tiny chapel, which is visited annually by some in their ranks who later immigrated to America. Arsonists twice set fire to the chapel in September 1999.

Indianapolis Star photo

V-J Day on Aug. 15, 1945, which marked the end of World War II, inspired a band of children to get out their flags and drums and stage a small but enthusiastic parade on an Indianapolis sidewalk (above).

Japan's surrender led some sailors to Indianapolis' Monument Circle, where they kissed every woman they could. Shortly after word arrived that the terms of surrender had been accepted, hundreds of people converged on the Circle.

Photo by Mike Fender

Lawrence Township students greeted soldiers returning from Operation Desert Storm during a parade
along East 56th Street on April 18, 1991. An estimated
6,000 people welcomed 230 Indiana-based Army re-
servists home from the conflict with Iraq, which became the target of a U.S.-led military coalition after
it invaded Kuwait on Aug. 2, 1990. The Persian Gulf
War was waged from Jan. 16 to Feb. 27, 1991, when
President George Bush declared Kuwait liberated.

An outburst by C. Allen Webster, father of an Arlington High junior who was asked to leave school until he shaved his mustache, brought an Indianapolis School Board meeting to a quick close Sept. 24, 1963. The matter was dropped without a vote.

Indianapolis police descended on Arlington High School on Sept. 30, 1991, the day that senior Bertram Bowman was fatally stabbed in the cafeteria by a friend after they scuffled. Officers also searched the campus that day for weapons that students may have tossed away when police arrived. The killer, Edward Ector, was convicted of voluntary manslaughter.

Competitors proved unable to stay out of each other's way during the 1956 White River Boat Race. Sponsored by the Central Indiana Boat Club, the race was run north of the West 30th Street bridge. *Indianapolis News* photographer George Tilford's shots of the crash won an Indiana Associated Press award.

Indianapolis Police Department diver Jerry Rieger (left) descends from a helicopter to rescue Jerry Herrington, 11, and Richard Lewchanin, 30, who were trapped in rapids on White River. The two had been cleaning trash and logs from the river on March 31, 1985, when the engine on their boat died.

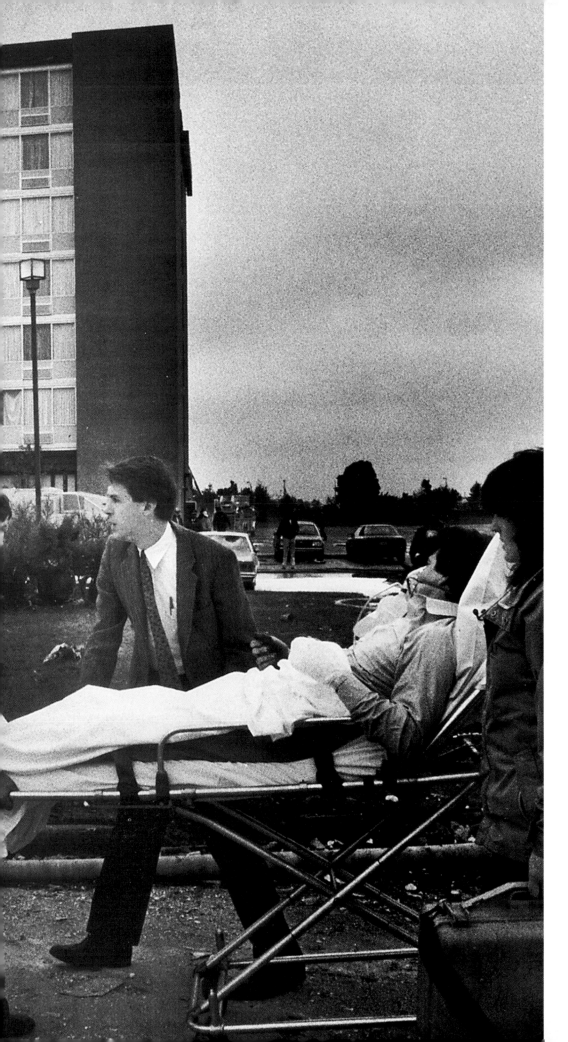

An injured man is wheeled to an ambulance after a military jet crashed into the Ramada Inn near Indianapolis International Airport. Ten people, most of them hotel employees, lost their lives in the accident on Oct. 20, 1987. After experiencing an engine flameout while attempting an emergency landing at the airport, Air Force Maj. Bruce Teagarden ejected from his A-7 Corsair, no longer able to control it. He parachuted to safety. The fighter jet struck the roof of a nearby bank building, hit the ground, skidded across a street and parking lot and slammed into the front of the Ramada. After sitting empty for several years, the hotel was demolished.

Photo by Mike Fender

37

Two private planes collided in midair in southeastern Marion County (above) on Sept. 11, 1992, killing Indianapolis civic leaders Frank McKinney Jr., Robert Welch, Michael Carroll and John Weliever and pilots William Mullen and William Bennett.

Photo by Joe Young

Florence Campbell of Bowling Green, Ohio, broke down after being reunited with 8-year-old daughter Elsie Mae at Indianapolis' bus station on Sept. 2, 1954 (right). They'd become separated the week before while hitchhiking from Arkansas to Ohio.

Photo by William Palmer

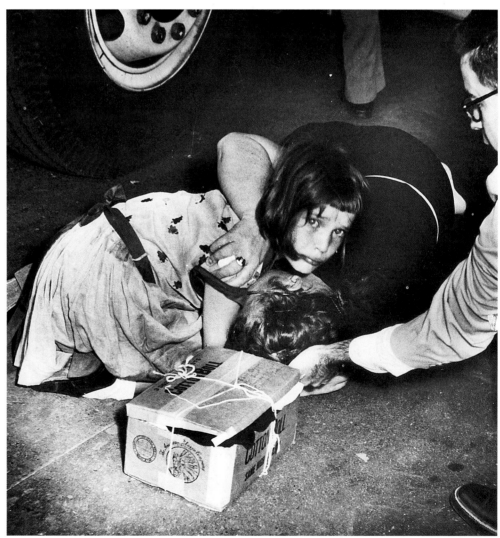

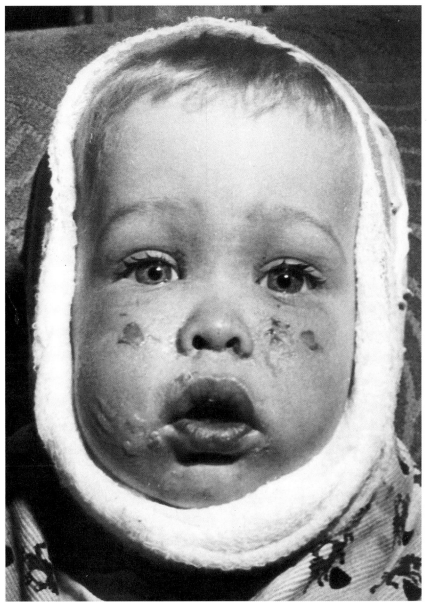

Published in *The Indianapolis News* in the 1957, this photograph of 18-month-old Scotty Fields, who had suffered burns on his head and face in a kitchen accident, was judged worthy of a first-place award in the Indiana Associated Press contest.

As if firefighters didn't have enough on their hands with a blaze at an Indianapolis lumberyard, their truck got stuck in mud and snow (below). It was one of 21 pieces of equipment used to fight the fire at Lindeman Wood Finish Co., 1602 W. Washington St., on Jan. 7, 1962.

Photo by George Tilford

Photo by Bob Doeppers

Photo by Patrick Schneider

Winds up to 30 mph made a difficult job all that much harder for Indianapolis firefighters summoned to the scene of a two-alarm blaze early on the morning of Feb. 21, 1995 (above). The fire destroyed 50 luxury condominiums that were being built in the 600 block of North West Street.

Photo by Mike Fender

Little remained of Hawcreek Missionary Baptist Church (above), near Hope in Bartholomew County, after an early morning fire on April 20, 1998. The 172-year-old church had served a congregation of 40. The blaze was ruled an arson, one of a series of church burnings in Indiana in 1997 and '98. The church's members hoped to rebuild.

Photo by Bob Doeppers

A general-alarm fire turned a historic stretch of Downtown Indianapolis into an inferno on Nov. 5, 1973. Firefighters and police officers hurried into office buildings, finding many people trapped. The multimillion-dollar blaze in the first block of East Washington Street started in the vacant W.T. Grant Building, which was being torn down. Three buildings were destroyed and 12 others were damaged; only six people were injured.

Photo by Matt Kryger

Leetha Glover (facing page) did the best she could as flames devoured a neighbor's home at 240 N. Davidson St. on Oct. 16, 1975. Much of the rear of the Near-Eastside house had been destroyed by the time firefighters arrived.

Photo by Bob Doeppers

A Wayne Township firefighter mans a hose (above) in the battle against a three-alarm blaze at Island Club Apartments on Indianapolis' Far Westside. Fourteen apartments were destroyed on March 18, 1999, and 17 people were left homeless. One firefighter was hospitalized with second- and third-degree burns.

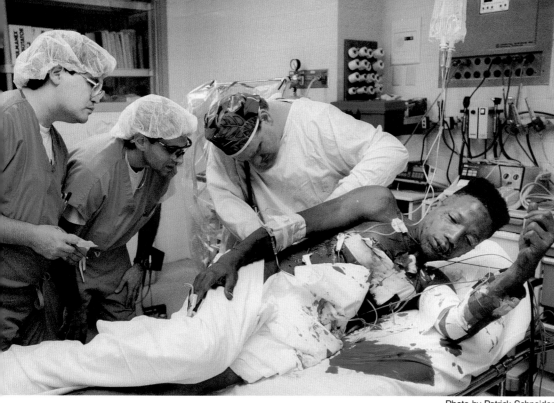

A young man who'd been cut with a straight-edge razor was taken care of by surgical residents Robert Binford, Mark Chaetsun and Dave Schindel (from left) in the fall of 1995 in the emergency room of Indianapolis' Wishard Memorial Hospital, the busiest one in the state.

Photo by Patrick Schneider

Photo by Joe Young

A severely burned tanker driver, Orval Hulley (facing page), crawls away from the truck after it exploded near St. Andrew Catholic Church on East 38th Street (left). A priest tried to help Hulley, who later died. Four others were killed in the inferno on Dec. 19, 1966.

Photo by Frank Fisse

An explosion and fire caused by leaking gas leveled part of downtown Richmond (above) on April 6, 1968. The disaster killed 41 people and destroyed 15 buildings. This view looks west over Sixth and Main; the Wayne County Courthouse is in the background.

Rev. Jesse Jackson (left in photo at right) honored local civil rights leader Rev. Andrew J. Brown with the PUSH Excellence Award on July 17, 1991. At right is Rev. T. Garrott Benjamin (now Bishop Benjamin) of Light of the World Christian Church.

Photo by Joe Young

Photo by Leroy Patton

Photo by Tim Halcomb

Supporters of the National Association for the Advancement of Colored People marched down Pennsylvania Street (above) on Aug. 4, 1963, to demand fairer treatment of blacks. The parade ended in a rally in University Park, where public officials and members of the integration movement addressed 3,000 people.

Presidential candidate Sen. Robert F. Kennedy (top right), shaken at news of Rev. Martin Luther King Jr.'s assassination on April 4, 1968, urged Indianapolis residents not to meet violence with violence. The next day, a memorial service for King was held on the Circle (lower right). On June 5, Kennedy was slain.

Photo by John Starkey

Voter Marguerite Bartholomew crossed paths with Shadow (below) as the cat returned to 65 S. Chester Ave., which doubled as a polling place on Dec. 3, 1985. Voters were deciding on a school referendum.

Photo by D. Todd Moore

The slow pace of voting gave Gena Sluss (left at table) and Debbie Sluss time for a game of dominoes, called Chickenfoot, on Nov. 7, 1995, at the St. Philip Neri School gym. It served as the polling place for Ward 10, Precinct 4.

Photo by Guy Reynolds

48

In January 1919, the Women's Franchise League of Indiana displayed petitions from its statewide drive for suffrage on the walls of its headquarters. On Jan. 16, 1920, Indiana ratified the 19th Amendment to the U.S. Constitution, which granted women the right to vote. However, it was not until 1921 that Indiana women were given the right to vote at the state level.

49

On April 11, 1965, Palm Sunday, the worst tornadoes in Indiana history killed more than 140 people and injured about 2,000. The Howard County towns of Greentown and Russiaville were heavily damaged. An aerial view (far left) shows the path of destruction through Greentown. In Marion, Mrs. Clifford Davis (at left) took in the sight of her daughter's house, which was destroyed that day. Her daughter survived.

Photos by Ed Lacey Jr.

51

Photos by J. Parke Randall

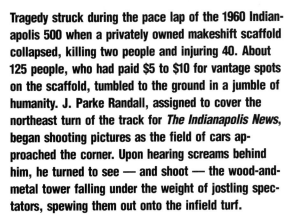

Tragedy struck during the pace lap of the 1960 Indianapolis 500 when a privately owned makeshift scaffold collapsed, killing two people and injuring 40. About 125 people, who had paid $5 to $10 for vantage spots on the scaffold, tumbled to the ground in a jumble of humanity. J. Parke Randall, assigned to cover the northeast turn of the track for *The Indianapolis News*, began shooting pictures as the field of cars approached the corner. Upon hearing screams behind him, he turned to see — and shoot — the wood-and-metal tower falling under the weight of jostling spectators, spewing them out onto the infield turf.

A crane removed wreckage after an explosion during an ice
show at the State Fairgrounds Coliseum on Oct. 31, 1963.
The blast, which killed 74, was touched off by gas leaking
from a propane tank near a popcorn warmer. The ice became
a temporary morgue for the blanket-covered bodies.

Photo by Joe Young

Newsmakers

People in the headlines often appear bigger than life. The photographic image has the power to do just that — transform a multifaceted personality into a one-dimensional icon. The camera lens may focus on a physical peculiarity, as with the world's tallest woman. Or it may accentuate an exceptional facet of a personality, such as a politician's presence. But newsmakers are far from one-dimensional. There are layers of complexity to their personalities. They are capable of great deeds or ignoble acts. Some fail to corral evil thoughts, and their names go down in history, forever tainted. Others, through an abundance of talent or vision, or sometimes a twist of fate, ascend to greatness. Photojournalists are among the first to encounter individuals destined for fame, people whose greatness has not yet been realized. When the lens is turned to such a person, public scrutiny is heightened. Many have risen to the challenge, not allowing celebrity to change them. And sadly, many have not.

Betty and Virgil I. "Gus" Grissom were welcomed by a crowd of 3,500 in their hometown of Mitchell on June 16, 1962, at festivities honoring the astronaut's accomplishments. Eleven months before, Grissom became the second American to be rocketed into space. In 1965, he became the first American to make two spaceflights when he and John Young made three orbits around Earth. Grissom died at the age of 40 on Jan. 27, 1967, in a fire in a space capsule at Cape Canaveral, Fla.

Photo by Robert A. Daugherty

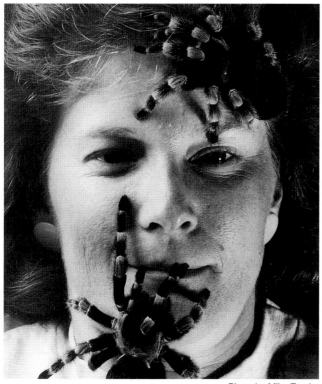

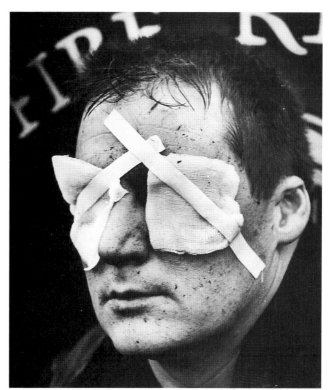

Photo by Mike Fender

Photo by William Palmer

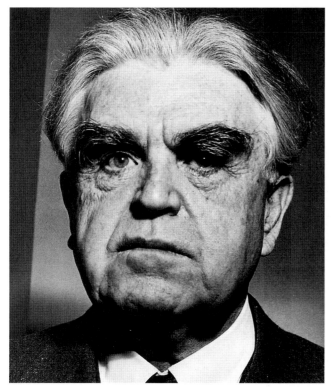

Photo by Robert Lavelle

Photo by Frank Espich

Tarantulas didn't bug Barbara Moore (top left), a science teacher at Warren Township's Creston Junior High School. She founded the American Tarantula Society in 1992.

United Mine Workers chief John Lewis (bottom left) visited Indianapolis on Dec. 20, 1947, for a dinner for Judge Oscar Bland. They worked together when Bland was in Congress.

Indianapolis firefighter Fred Eichrodt Jr. (top right) was burned about the eyes and face in an apartment building blaze on Feb. 21, 1962. Eichrodt, 34, recovered in a week.

Olympic gold medalist Gail Devers (bottom right) showed off all-natural nails on April 16, 1997, at an Indianapolis news conference about the U.S. Track and Field Championships.

A 140-degree 120 Panon camera peeking through curtains, unnoticed by the Secret Service, observed presidential candidate Sen. John F. Kennedy (below) at the State Fairgrounds Coliseum on Oct. 4, 1960.

In 1958, young Evan Bayh hit the books under the eye of his mother, Marvella, and father, state Rep. Birch Bayh. Dad went on to become a U.S. senator from 1963 to 1981. Son Evan served as Indiana governor before following in his father's footsteps: He became a U.S. senator in 1999.

Indianapolis Star photo

Elwood native Wendell Willkie (above) and his wife, Edith (right), relaxed for a while in the shade of a sycamore tree on Aug. 17, 1940; the following day, he accepted the Republican presidential nomination.

Sen. Dan Quayle (right) visited Cleveland with Vice President George Bush after the 1988 Republican National Convention. The candidates for president and vice president previously stopped in Huntington, Quayle's hometown.

Photo by Rich Miller

Photo by Jeff Atteberry

Ryan White (above) looked like a typical 14-year-old in his Kokomo bedroom. But Ryan, a hemophiliac diagnosed with AIDS in 1984, lived his teen years in the spotlight. He was just 18 when he died in 1990.

Rock star Elton John (above) played his song *Skyline Pigeon* for White's funeral at Second Presbyterian Church in Indianapolis. Singer Michael Jackson and talk show host Phil Donahue also attended.

Indianapolis Star photo

While Stateside on Sept. 13, 1944, war correspondent and Dana native Ernie Pyle returned to the newspaper office at Indiana University, where he spent his college days, and read the latest news about the war.

Impressionist painter T.C. (Theodore Clement) Steele painted a landscape near Bloomington (facing page) in this photo published by *The Indianapolis Star* on May 31, 1925. Steele, born in 1847 in Owen County, operated a portrait studio in Indianapolis during the latter part of the 1800s. In 1907, enamored with landscapes, he bought 211 acres of wooded property in Brown County. He died in 1926.

Indianapolis Star photo

When heart transplant patient Louis B. Russell Jr. (above) came home after his Aug. 24, 1968, surgery, his daughter Helen was prepared. The teacher was the world's longest-surviving heart recipient at the time of his death in 1974.

Vincennes native Red Skelton (right) hammed it up on Aug. 30, 1962, at the State Fair, where he gave five performances. The comedian was CBS' Tuesday night hit from 1953 to 1970. Richard Bernard Skelton died in 1997 at 84.

Author Kurt Vonnegut Jr., a 1940 graduate of Short-ridge High School, visited his hometown of Indianapolis on April 1, 1965, the week before the release of his novel *God Bless You, Mr. Rosewater.* Four years later, *Slaughterhouse Five* made him a guru of the counterculture because of its anti-war theme.

Photo by Bob Doeppers

Indianapolis News photo

Amelia Earhart (above) came to Indianapolis on May 29, 1935, to officiate at the 500-Mile Race, the first woman to do so. That same year, the aviator became a part-time staff member at Purdue University. In 1932, Earhart was the first woman to fly solo across the Atlantic. She was on leave from the university in 1937 when her plane (dubbed the Purdue Flying Laboratory) disappeared over the Pacific during an attempted around-the-world flight.

Photo by Joseph E. Craven

Booth Tarkington and his wife, Susannah — and Figaro — returned to Indianapolis on Jan. 6, 1938, after eight months away. The author of *The Magnificent Ambersons* and *Alice Adams* won two Pulitzers.

Indianapolis Mayor William Hudnut joined in the celebration of the Gaither quintuplets' fifth birthday on Aug. 3, 1988. Brandon, Joshua, Renee, Ashlee and Rhealyn (from left) were the first quints born in Indiana.

Photo by Tim Halcomb

Curious toddlers gathered around Sandy Allen, 19, (left) on Dec. 3, 1974. The 7-foot-7¼-inch Chicago native, who moved to Shelbyville as a young girl, is listed in the *Guinness Book of Records* as the tallest living woman.

Photo by Patty Espich

Youngsters received a special Indiana history lesson on May 15, 1916, at the Indianapolis home of poet James Whitcomb Riley. With Lockerbie on his lap, Riley told of the state's past in a documentary for the Indiana Centennial. He died two months later at 66.

Robert Indiana was there in February 1972 as his LOVE sculpture was placed outside the Indiana National Bank tower. The artwork later moved to the Indianapolis Museum of Art. The Hoosier changed his last name because "it's easier to make a unique contribution if you have a unique name."

Photo by Tim Halcomb

Actor Richard Gere (left) and retired IU Professor Thubten Norbu were among the thousands taking part in the Kalachakra Initiation in August 1999. The 2,400-year-old Buddhist teaching was conducted in Bloomington by the Dalai Lama, Tibet's exiled leader and Norbu's younger brother.

Photo by Robert Scheer

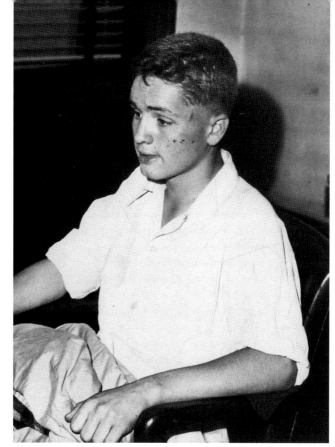

Two notorious men with Indianapolis-area backgrounds are Charles Manson (upper left) and Jim Jones (lower left). On Oct. 19, 1949, 14-year-old Manson was back in custody for attempted burglary after escaping from the Indiana Boys School near Plainfield. At 16, he escaped again and drove a stolen car to California, where he later founded his "family" in San Francisco's Haight-Ashbury. Manson and three female followers were sentenced to death for the Aug. 9, 1969, murders of actress Sharon Tate and six others; the sentences later were reduced to life in prison. On Dec. 7, 1953, Jones (left) posed with Sugar, one of the monkeys sold in a church fund-raiser. Jones built a following of believers in Indianapolis, where he founded Peoples Temple Full Gospel Church in the 1950s. On Nov. 18, 1978, Jones and 900 of his followers committed mass suicide in Jonestown, Guyana, by drinking Kool-Aid laced with cyanide.

Seymour native and hitmaker John Mellencamp, performing as Johnny Cougar (left), made his official world debut in the Seymour armory in October 1976 after recording his first album, *Chestnut Street Incident*.

Photo by Zach Dunkin

Kenneth "Babyface" Edmonds (right) returned to Indianapolis in July 1999 for a ceremony at which a 17-mile stretch of I-65 was named in his honor. He has written, produced or performed more than 50 hit songs.

Photo by Matt Detrich

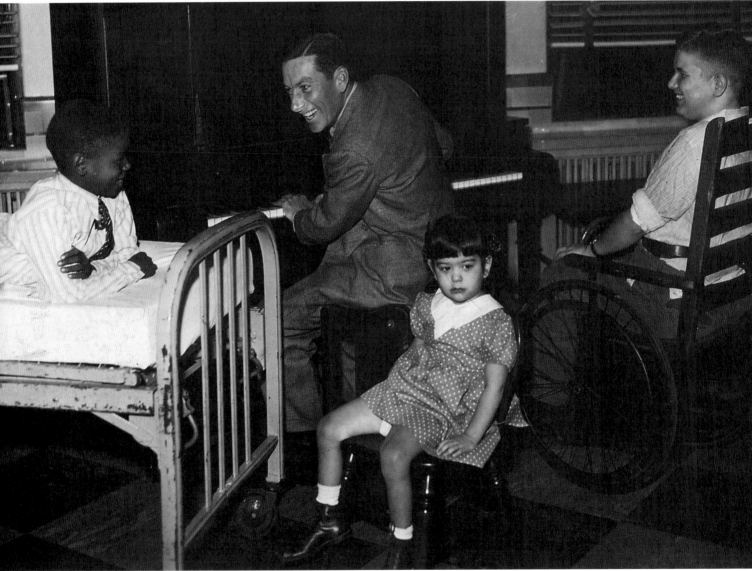

Indianapolis Star photo

Hoosier composer and singer Hoagy Carmichael performed several tunes for young patients at Riley Hospital on Jan. 29, 1942. Carmichael, who wrote such songs as *Star Dust* and *Georgia On My Mind*, was in Indianapolis for a show the next day at Butler Fieldhouse. He died in 1981.

As Richard Lugar's first year as Indianapolis mayor was winding down on Dec. 27, 1968, the Indiana National Bank tower was going up blocks from his City-County Building office. Lugar, a native of Indianapolis, was a member of the Indianapolis Public School Board before serving as mayor from 1968 to 1976. The Republican was elected to the U.S. Senate that bicentennial year.

Photo by John Starkey

Photo by Joe Young

Indianapolis Mayor John Barton (above) demonstrated his cooking skills at the Mayor's Breakfast on May 21, 1964. The Democrat was mayor from 1964 to 1968, losing his bid for re-election to Richard Lugar. At right, then-Prosecutor Stephen Goldsmith teamed with Spiderman on April 1, 1986, to fight child abuse. Goldsmith, a Republican, was elected mayor in 1991 and re-elected in 1995.

Photo by Patty Espich

CHAPTER 3

Photo by William Palmer

Earning a Buck

The economic expansion in Indiana at the end of the 20th century in many ways echoed the expansion of the post-Civil War years. Indianapolis' central location in a rich agricultural belt, proximity to inexpensive fuel coal in southern Indiana and a highly developed land transportation system propelled the city into industrial prominence. In the early 1900s, auto builders based in Indianapolis turned out cars under the brands of Stutz, Marmon and Cole. As the automotive industry shifted to Detroit, Indianapolis became a leader in production of auto parts and transportation equipment. In the 1960s, booming highway and building construction provided not only plenty of jobs, but also the infrastructure for future development. The 1990s saw the revitalization of Downtown, with such additions as Circle Centre, Victory Field and the Conseco Fieldhouse, home of the Indiana Pacers.

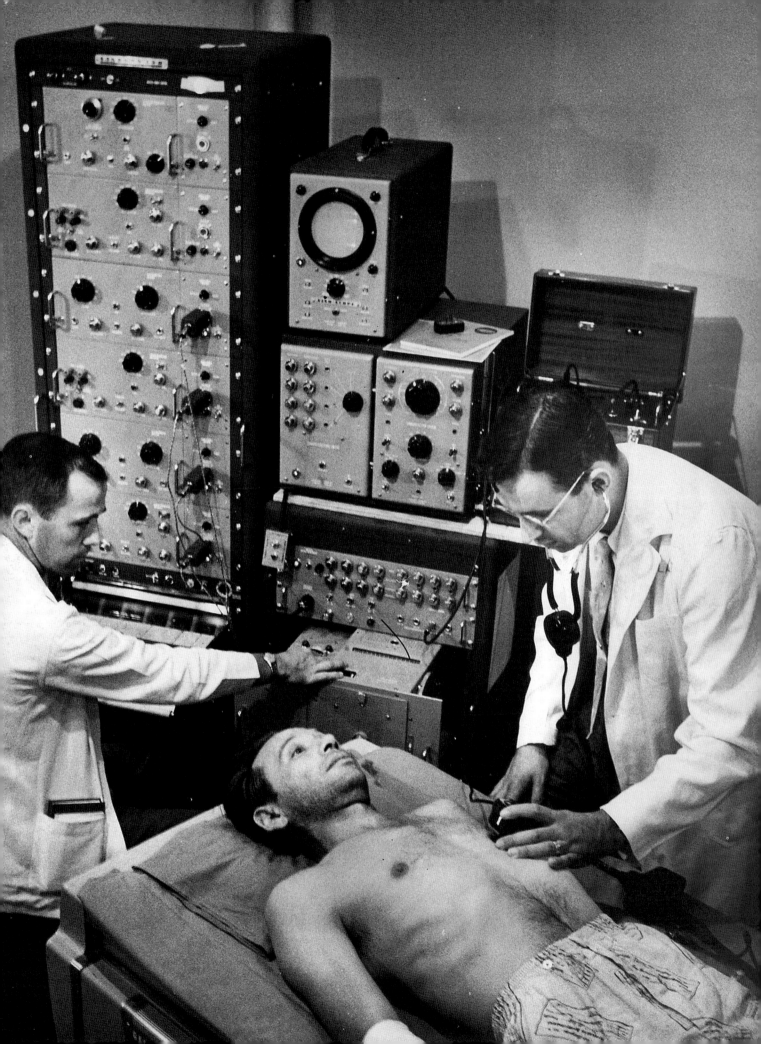

Miners at Victory Mine (right), 11 miles east of Terre Haute, were back at work Nov. 10, 1949, after a 52-day strike over the United Mine Workers' welfare and retirement fund. Victory Mine operated as an underground coal mine from 1943 to 1954.

Photo by Paul Shideler

On Oct. 29, 1953, a Stop & Shop salesman in Indianapolis tried to convince a mother of the advantages of owning a television set (below). By 1953, more than 137,000 sets were in Indianapolis homes.

Photo by Dale Schofner

Emmagee Washington, a visitor to Indiana Black Expo '73, looked over a line of makeup exhibited by Dorothy Sales (left) and Judy Sales. First held in June 1971, Expo celebrates black history and achievement. It has expanded into a weeklong event featuring seminars, an employment fair and entertainment.

Photo by Jim Young

In 1951, Cory SerVaas had cornered a piece of the market with the Cory Jane Clamp-on Apron. That invention was followed by others, including the plastic bib worn by son Eric. The wife of future City-County Council President Beurt SerVaas later became editor and publisher of *The Saturday Evening Post*.

Photo by Joseph Craven

73

Massive engines were all in a day's work at the Beech Grove train shops near the start of the century. The rail yard, which once employed about 5,000, began in 1908 as shops for the Cleveland, Cincinnati, Chicago & St. Louis Railway. The work force had dropped to 950 by the end of 1998, when the Amtrak-operated facility won its first contract in years to overhaul rail cars for another railroad. The passenger rail system hoped the deal would be the first in a series of profit-making ventures to help wean it from federal operating subsidies.

Indianapolis News photo

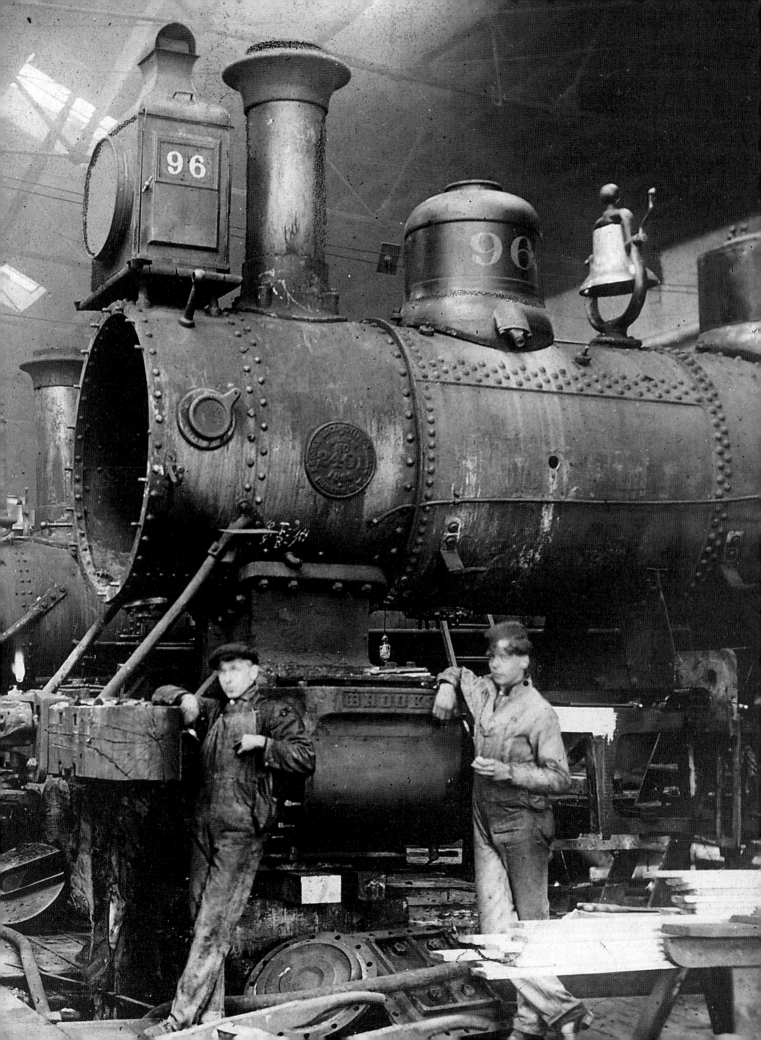

Eli Lilly and Co. employees had another workday under their belts on Oct. 11, 1956, crossing at McCarty and Alabama streets in Indianapolis. A new intersection control system stopped all traffic, letting pedestrians cross in all directions. It was activated in the morning, at noon and in the evening.

Indianapolis street vendor Nicholas Marianos (left) satisfied the public's appetite for candy, popcorn and peanuts from his cart on Vermont Street between Pennsylvania and Meridian streets on April 12, 1950. Marianos also operated The Star Restaurant, a Greek eatery at 333 W. Washington St. He died in 1971 at 99.

Photo by William Myers

Drug packages were assembled on the Eli Lilly and Co. insulin finishing line on Jan. 26, 1937. In 1922, Lilly signed an agreement with the University of Toronto to become the sole U.S. supplier of insulin.

Alda Ulsass, whose stand specialized in unusual foods and brands, chatted with longtime customer Mike Terpinas at the City Market on Feb. 10, 1964. Behind her was her son Tom. Some market stands have been operated by the same families for years.

Hoosier workers put the finishing touches on trucks at the Marmon-Herrington plant in 1952. Working on the assembly line in Indianapolis on March 11 of that year were Jim Young, John Gellert, Bob Leslie, Art Winburn and Claude Snider. (One man is not visible.)

Photo by Robert Lavelle

The 1970s presented new opportunities for women in the workplace, including jobs that had been the domain of men. Sue Bear of Lawrenceburg, working construction on July 24, 1975, headed up a wall.

Another purchase in the basket, Mary Roberts maneuvered the delivery device up and away on April 1, 1965. At the Downtown Stout's store, customers' shoes and money are sent to a cashier on the second floor.

Detroit's Camille Rodwell (left) introduced visitors to the Plymouth exhibit at the 1973 Indianapolis Automobile Show on Jan. 4. The display explained modifications to the Aspen's engine to produce cleaner exhaust. The event drew more than 100,000 people.

CHAPTER 4

Photo by Joe Young

Having someone to share the household expenses saves money, but the laughs and companionship can be just as valuable. When Bertha Miller (left) decided in July 1988 that she needed a boarder to ease her financial burden, she turned to Homemates and found Violet Cox. The shared-housing program for senior citizens was offered at Hawthorne Community Center.

The People

Forget stereotypes when you think of Hoosiers. There aren't any simple answers about which traits they share. What, for example, does a double-amputee war veteran have in common with a boy selected from Brown County for a movie role because he looked like the young Babe Ruth? And what traits do they share with a 3-year-old South Korean immigrant receiving her naturalization papers? All are Hoosiers, and probably proud of it. Yet even with this diversity of the state's residents — 5.8 million at the close of the 20th century — some traits seem ingrained in the Hoosier character. The people of Indiana are hard-working and patriotic, committed to their faith and to one another. They are generally a modest bunch; and, smack dab in the heart of the country, they think of themselves as typical Americans.

Photo by Mike Fender

Harold Goodpasture, 72, practiced his backward, be-
tween-the-knees shot from 44 feet out on May 9,
1995. Some days, he'd spend an hour launching 40 or
50 shots, hitting three to eight. The Charlottesville
man died six months after this photo was taken.

81

First Baptist Church (above) was a busy place on Good Friday 1950. It moved from Meridian and Vermont streets to 8600 North College Ave. in 1960.

Photo by Paul Shideler

Indianapolis radio evangelist B.M. Page's tattered Bible was still serving its purpose well in October 1989. *What the Bible Says* had aired on WIBC since 1953.

Photo by Gary Moore

Ahkilah Al-Thaaquib of Indianapolis was a study in Muslim spirituality in this photo from a July 19, 1997, story on Indiana Black Expo's Summer Celebration, which draws participants from varied ethnic groups and religions.

Photo by Rich Miller

HASTEN HEBREW A

Students at Hasten Hebrew Academy of Indianapolis (above) squeeze in a bit more sightseeing on Monument Circle before leaving. Having fun on May 6, 1999, were (from left) Melinda Bruner, Esther Margolis, Braca Benizry, Megan Brattain, Ashley Hanson (elbows out window) and Rachel Farahan.

Photo by Patty Espich

Outside St. Mary Catholic Church, 11-year-old Ixchel Vargas (right) awaits a big moment in her life. She and 16 other young people received their first Communion on May 2, 1999, during a special Hispanic Mass at the sanctuary in Indianapolis.

Photo by Frank Espich

83

The fit is tight, but the look is classic — Ford's 1964½ Mustang. Ken Schmidt's pedal car (right, in 1994) is 39 inches long and 14 inches high. He headed Blue Diamond Classics of Indianapolis, a pedal car parts remanufacturer and distributor.

Nashville fifth-grader Andy Voils (below) demonstrated his style on May 1, 1991, after winning the role of a young Babe Ruth in the 1992 film *The Babe.* Andy arrived for the audition in knickers, suspenders and cap; none of the other boys had dressed up.

Photo by Mike Fender

Photo by Paul Sancya

The Houck family (left) was in the spotlight for a Father's Day story on June 16, 1963. At the dinner table are (from left) Elizabeth, 4; Emerson, with Joseph, 2½; and Jane. Emerson Houck worked in the office of a local manufacturing company.

Photo by Ed Lacey Jr.

Indianapolis News photo

A 64-year-old woman, paralyzed from the hips down, supported herself, her disabled husband and her epileptic daughter by taking in washing. *The Indianapolis News* appealed for contributions on Dec. 12, 1912.

Nevils and Juanita Shedd (right), who met at Indianapolis' All Souls Unitarian Church in 1963 and were among very few interracial married couples of the day, had their commitment tested over the years. They were photographed on Valentine's Day 1995.

Photo by Rich Miller

85

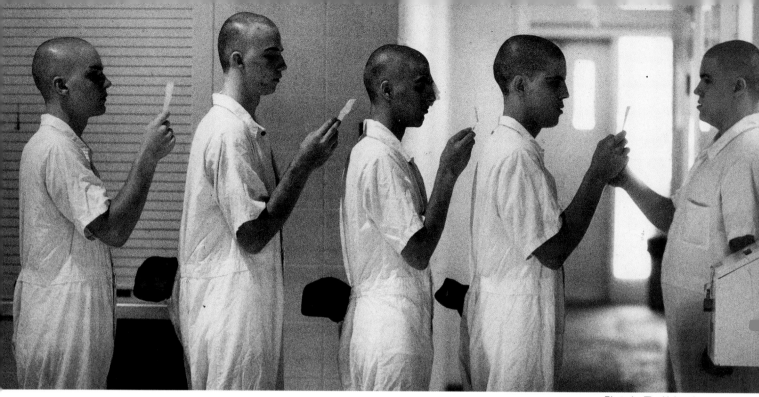

Photo by Tim Halcomb

Probationers (above) study "boot camp" rules at Michigan's Camp Sauble, visited by an Indiana legislative study panel in October 1989. Camp Summit opened at Pinhook, in northern Indiana, in 1995.

Among the traits that 4-year-old Cody and Wendell Crook share is the way they wear their hair (below). This photo of the Beech Grove pair was among a gallery of parent-and-child look-alikes published in *The Indianapolis Star* on Feb. 19, 1995.

Photo by Patty Espich

In July 1996, Connie McDavid of Carmel (above) preferred the natural look after losing her hair to cancer treatment. "I felt weird in a wig . . . phony," she said in a story about a program helping women with cancer take control through their appearance.

Photo by Rob Goebel

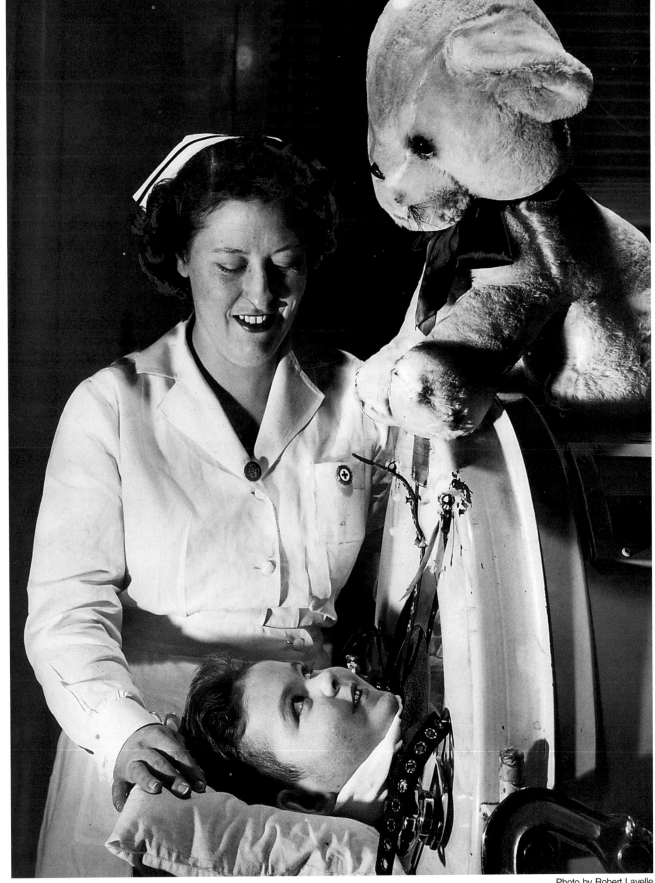

Forced to rely on an iron lung, 6-year-old Tommy Burgner managed a smile for nurse Gertrude Nichel at Riley Hospital on Feb. 23, 1950. The Veedersburg boy, who fell ill in a 1949 polio epidemic, died at age 12.

Photo by Jeff Atteberry

John Morton-Finney (above), a 105-year-old World War I veteran, was a highlight of the 1994 Veterans Day parade in Indianapolis. The Kentucky native, an Indianapolis Public Schools teacher for 47 years, earned 11 bachelor's degrees and five law degrees. He died on Jan. 28, 1998, at the age of 108.

The Defense Savings Bond rally in Indianapolis on Jan. 15, 1942, starred actress Carole Lombard (right), a Fort Wayne native. She is shown with future *Star* and *News* owner and publisher Eugene C. Pulliam (left) and Will H. Hays (center), president of Motion Picture Producers and Distributors of America. Lombard, the wife of actor Clark Gable, died the next day in a plane crash.

Photo by Bob Hoover

Inducted into the Army at 19 in early 1943, Chet Perkins (right) lost his eyesight while laying mines in Germany. On Nov. 6, 1991, he showed a snapshot of himself in uniform that first year in the service. Perkins retired as public relations manager of the American Lung Association of Central Indiana.

Photo by Mike Fender

Michael Douglas, AMVETS state commander for Indiana, saluted during the posting of the colors at the 1988 Veterans Day ceremonies in Downtown Indianapolis. About 400 veterans and their families gathered in brilliant sunshine at the 11th hour of the 11th day of the 11th month, the time of the formal conclusion of World War I in 1918. Douglas of Alexandria — whose organization's name is short for American Veterans of World War II, Korea and Vietnam — lost both legs to a land mine in Vietnam in 1969.

Photo by Tim Halcomb

89

Photo by Steve Healey

Ovellar Forte (above) gazes out the window of her room at Alpha Home. The 95-year-old woman often got tired of being told what to do, but "they ain't mean," she said of nursing home staff on May 6, 1998.

Her name was Sadie and she used to sit and watch life in the 400 block of Massachusetts Avenue in Indianapolis in the early '70s. That's about all that was known about her; and when this photo (right) was taken, she didn't reveal any more.

Photo by Patty Espich

Jill Leeper (right), a Butler University faculty member, was completing a doctorate in American literature when photographed with her "Tribal Tattoo" on Oct. 30, 1998. The ex-farm girl is also a keyboardist.

Photo by Patty Espich

Three-year-old Rachael Voss (above), a native of South Korea, stayed close by as her dad signed her naturalization papers on March 10, 1987. Earl and Brenda Voss of Seymour adopted Rachael in 1985.

George Stevens (right), a sophomore at Indianapolis' Manual High School, rested his chin on his foot during English class on May 20, 1998. Stevens was born without arms, but he manages to take notes, eat and work on computers with his feet.

Oliver "Ding Dong" Bell (above), doorkeeper of the Indiana Senate, greeted senators with "Hi, Chief!" Bell, who retired in 1974 after 15 years, was photographed on Jan. 8 of that year. After he died in '78, other doorkeepers began wearing boutonnieres.

91

Samuel Oliver Crane uses coal-oil lamps outdoors and inside his 1843 brick house in southeastern Shelby County. The house, which he bought in 1988 for $10,000, has no electricity or running water, and that's fine with Crane: He has his books, his Victrola, his pets and none of the stresses of modern living. Baths are taken in a tub in the kitchen; it takes two hours to heat enough water on his wood stove, which also serves to heat up the iron. In '99 Crane, 61, said he's "always been pointed in a backward direction."

| CHAPTER 5 |

The Heartland

Although Indiana's landscape lacks an outstanding geographic centerpiece, such as a mountain range or grand waterway, the region's beauty is unmistakable. It is seen in the expanse of rich farmland and dense tracts of woods, which provide a respite from the maze of streets and crisscrossing interstates of the cities. Lush fields of crops adorn the countryside; at their peak, Indiana's cornfields take on an aura of art, their exact rows stretching to the horizon. There is solace in the countryside's peace and quiet. The pace of life is slower. The soil has been planted year after year with soybeans, wheat and corn — for many, a ritual that transcends generations.

But the expansion of city boundaries has touched the farm families who have been wedded to their land for years. To some, their farmland has become a gold mine. To others, selling out is not an option. The land is part of them, and the great, open expanses of fields are a source of their strength — as they will be for years to come.

Drew Price found just enough room for a view amid Stonycreek Farm's pumpkins (above). He and his parents, Andy and Teresa Price of Lebanon, were visiting the popular site near Noblesville on Oct. 14, 1994.

City folks sampled country living in July 1963 (right), courtesy of Wendell and Belva Stapp, who offered vacations at their farm south of Greensburg. Visitors ate meals with the family, fed lambs and took pony rides.

Indianapolis Star Photo

Photo by Tim Halcomb

Boone County 4-H Fair Queen Julie Zarse, 20, and her court were on stage to judge the Hog Calling Contest on July 23, 1998; but a pile of manure from the last show was odorous, so Zarse took action (above). Also handy with a shovel is Henry Bontrager (right) of Ontario, Ind. — like most Amish, he shuns technology. October 1993 found him picking corn by hand, shucking ears and tossing them into a horse-drawn wagon.

Photo by Guy Reynolds

In Johnson County, Lloyd and Martha Keller's tomato plants were having a great year in 1994. A path among them was good ground for horseshoes.

John H. Lightle (above), who farmed 37 acres on U.S. 52 near Thorntown in Boone County, used a three-horse team and a drag to prepare a seed bed for his corn crop in May 1950. The horses, Dolly, May and King, were about 15 years old.

Isaac Drew, 94, may have been Indiana's oldest working farmer when he was photographed climbing over a fence to get to his grain bin in Washington County on Oct. 15, 1996 (right). Drew began farming in 1937.

A 1947 tornado took the roof off the round barn at Everett Gruber's Carroll County farm. The barn was warped, so engineers recommended a conventional roof for it's replacement. Gruber is pictured in 1992.

Photo by Rob Goebel

Photo by Frank Espich

"I enjoy watching things grow and multiply," hog farmer Bob Kissel, based in New Palestine, said in a *Star/News* photographic tribute to Labor Day 1995.

Indianapolis Star photo

In April 1942, Roy Kearns (above) was readying ground at his dad's farm at 30th Street and Tibbs Avenue for tomato plants to help meet the demand during WWII.

Two-year-old Keegan McCamment (right) of Greensburg got in on the action, albeit on a smaller scale, as dad Larry drove the family tractor in a parade at the 1987 State Fair.

Photo by Joe Young

Photo by Guy Reynolds

Eric Mohr (above left) joins his father, Ronnie, for a tailgate lunch of pot roast served up by his mother, Sarah, at their farm in Hancock County. The corn harvest in late October 1993 brought workdays that began early and ended after dark.

A good supply of water was a must under the blazing sun of July 1960, as Ottis Augsburger of Indianapolis (left) and George Henderson of Shelbyville could attest. They were taking a break atop a wagon full of wheat ready to go through the separator.

Photo by Larry George

Rain was needed in August 1952, but Milton Smith (center) hoped it would stay dry until his Korean lespedeza was in the barn. Helping on the farm at Sulphur were Samuel Wright (left) and Alva Armstrong.

Photo by Frank Espich

Old-time maple syrup maker Arch Foxworthy (left) checked on the latest batch of sugar water boiling away in a rural Parke County sugar shack on March 2, 1999. The sugar water would become the amber liquid known as 100 percent maple syrup, Indiana-style. Near Gnaw Bone on Ind. 46, a 1-horsepower press (right) squeezed the sap from the stalks at a sorghum mill on Sept. 10, 1972, to produce sorghum molasses. It was one of the few old-time mills still operating in the United States.

Photo by Horace Ketring

It was a full pull for
Grandpa's Pride Train (left)
at the 1990 State Fair
when Art Moorman of Sey-
mour and his grandkids
paraded by. A full basket
of melons was what Tim
Spurgeon (above) had on
his hands at an Indianapolis farmers' market in '89.

Another long day on the farm for Eric Mohr (above) included a trip to an implement dealer for a new drive
belt. The Mohrs were laboring long and hard in October 1993 to harvest their corn in Hancock County.

CHAPTER 6

Photo by Patty Espich

Fashion Statements

Photo by William Palmer

Kelly Rackley, Michelle Ellington, Jennifer Carter, Karyn Weaver and Tammy Buckner (top, from left), of Indianapolis' Decatur Central, wore "black and white in a fun new way" in 1988. The 1950s' classic duo was hat (with veil) and gloves.

Fashion is and always has been a reflection of its time. Changing political winds, world events and shifting social mores find an outlet in the clothing with which Hoosiers, as well as others throughout the country, choose to adorn themselves. Evolving concepts of fashion and beauty mark the 20th century as one whose society has undergone radical change. As the century opened, modesty was a defining ideal, with ground-grazing skirts the hallmarks of a fashionable lady's dress. But over the decades, fashions swung from one extreme to the other — from miniskirts to maxi-skirts, from pantsuits to hot pants. The Teen Rebellion look of the Fifties was offset by serious, grown-up, old-money looks in the Eighties. At the dawn of the new millennium, clothing choices are more numerous than ever. Nineties fashion saw practically every kind of throwback imaginable, from '60s tie-dye to '70s platform shoes, '40s Hollywood style and the '50s cocktail-lounge scene. Never before was fashion so in search of a towering trend as it was at the end of the century.

In 1952, Laurel (Ind.) High School officials encouraged students to wear jeans because they were economical. Jean Ann Poe, Sharon Wicker and Sharon Kay Steffey (from left) didn't need much encouragement.

Photo by Rob Goebel

Prison stripes actually can be a great escape outfit, if you're fleeing across the 500 Festival Parade's checkered carpet. This Keystone Kops takeoff was part of the 1992 Downtown extravaganza on May 23.

Photo by Jim Young

The word in 1970 was that the miniskirt was giving way to the "midi." That word apparently hadn't reached Indianapolis. An assigned search for someone wearing the calf-length skirt came up short.

Pedestrians moved briskly across Meridian Street one sunny afternoon in February 1923 (below), when proper winter attire included long black coats and hats for men, women and children alike. This was the view looking north from Washington Street.

Indianapolis Star photo

Fort Wayne native Bill Blass (near right), who cut a sharp figure while talking to reporters about his spring collection in 1997, became famous for incorporating menswear themes into tailored, feminine styles. Among his fans are former first lady Nancy Reagan and TV newswoman Barbara Walters. Blass' first collection was modeled at L.S. Ayres & Co. in 1958. Businesswomen in 1995 found the new "power pantsuit" (far right) a comfortable but still stylish alternative to the skirt suit.

Photo at near right by Patty Espich

Photo at far right by Frank Espich

Photo by Ron Ira Steele

For men's heads, styles have swung from covered to creative. Kevin Winterberg opted for straight-up at 1995's Sloppypalooza punk rock festival in Indianapolis (left). A variation on the vertical theme was modeled by Anthony Powell of Detroit at a hair design show in the capital city in 1993. But in the century's early years, hats were the norm. Dr. Harvey Wiley (below), who helped get the Pure Food and Drug Act passed, sported a derby in 1912.

Photo by Frank Espich

Indianapolis News photo

Years ago, cartoonists had fun with the stereotype of the hard-to-please female shoe buyer. In 1950, *The Indianapolis Star* got three salesmen's opinions. One found women more reasonable than men; one said shoes were a woman's hardest fashion decision. The third said men could be just as hard to please.

Photo by Frank Fisse

Good ol' denim (below) was hailed as *the* look for fall and winter of 1987. Stone-washed, acid-washed, colors other than blue; jackets, jumpsuits, skirts. "The miracle fabric of the age," designer Calvin Klein declared. "Denim has been very hot," a marketing executive for The Limited concurred.

Photo by David Eulitt

Flora Jefferson (below) opened Flora's Unique Boutique at 16 W. 22nd St. in 1991. Photographed in her 10th year of business, she credited her success to the prayers of the church ladies among her clientele.

Photo by Mike Fender

Mrs. William Spence (right) reflected the styles of the day in this photo from May 1931. Her husband, a race car driver, had been killed in the 10th lap of Indianapolis 500-Mile Race on May 30, 1929, when his Duesenberg hit the southeast wall and overturned.

Indianapolis Star photo

The power of red —
"There are no hidden
meanings here: Passion
and potency are directly
communicated" — was
the subject of a holiday
fashion report in November
1995 that featured model
Staci Lipscomb, radiant in
a silk ball gown (right).

Photo by Patty Espich

A fire drill on Dec. 12,
1958, at Wood High School
also provided a look at Indianapolis high school
fashions (left). Teens practiced evacuations of the
school at 501 S. Meridian
St. for several months,
then won first place
among city high schools
for the best fire drills.

Photo by Larry George

How to make an outfit
work for both a day at the
office and the holiday-sea-
son party that night was
timely information on Dec.
5, 1998. Model Angela
Hogg (right) demonstrates
what can be done with
your basic black dress
when you keep it simple.

Photo by Frank Espich

CHAPTER 7

Photo by Paul Sancya

The Indiana Pacers' Rik Smits battles for a rebound with the Chicago Bulls' Michael Jordan and Dennis Rodman (right) in Game 3 of 1998's Eastern Conference finals at Market Square Arena. Indiana won that May 23 game, 107-105. The Bulls went on to win the series, though, with an 88-83 victory in the seventh game. Chicago later captured its sixth National Basketball Association title, defeating the Utah Jazz in six games.

The Sporting Spirit

For decades, Indianapolis has been synonymous with auto racing — specifically the Indianapolis 500, the largest one-day sporting event in the world. But the city and state lay claim to more than the "Greatest Spectacle in Racing." Indiana has been home to legendary greats of the 20th century, including Notre Dame's Knute Rockne, NBA phenom Larry Bird and track and field star Wilma Rudolph. While auto racing and basketball command the majority of attention among Indiana's athletic interests, organized sports on all levels have been embraced by Hoosiers. And throughout the years, photographers have excited readers by capturing the drama of athletes in action. Sport isn't just about winning: It's about the thrill of competition, the fulfillment of dreams and the pursuit of excellence.

Photo by George Tilford

Future NBA legend Oscar Robertson returned in 1958 to visit Crispus Attucks, the all-black Indianapolis school he led to state basketball titles in 1955 and '56. The Hall of Famer is now a Cincinnati business-man.

A vocal Bobby "Slick" Leonard (near right) let his players — and referees — know how he felt while coaching the Indiana Pacers in 1976, during their American Basketball Association days. Slick continues to be vocal as the Pacers' radio color man. John Wooden (far right), shown at Hinkle Fieldhouse in 1994, coached UCLA to 10 national titles in 12 years. He began his basketball career by leading Martinsville High to the state championship in '27.

Photo by Jeff Atteberry

Photo by Mike Fender

Photo by Mike Fender

It was on March 19, 1995, at Market Square Arena that Michael Jordan returned to the NBA after a two-year absence and a fling with baseball. NBC's Ahmad Rashad interviewed him after his Bulls lost to Indiana.

You don't need a hoop and backboard to develop nice moves (facing page); these youngsters made do in an alley behind their Indianapolis home in the mid-1980s.

Photo by D. Todd Moore

Indiana University basketball coach Bob Knight demonstrated his fiery temper (left) after Jim Wisman's miscues displeased him in a game against Michigan in 1976. Wisman got a lecture on the bench. IU won, 72-67, and capped its 32-0 season with a national championship the next month.

Photo by Jerry Clark

Photo by Rich Miller

Another side of coach Knight's personality is evident in a teary embrace of his son, Patrick, on Senior Night at Bloomington's Assembly Hall (above). Patrick had just been taken out of the game with 38.5 seconds left on March 12, 1995, and walked over to his dad for a hug. Eight years earlier, joy reigned as Steve Alford and teammates hoisted the NCAA trophy (right) after the Hoosiers won a fifth national title.

Photo by John Gentry

George McGinnis, Washington High School's All-State basketball superstar, was surrounded by a trio of Silver Creek players during a game at Hinkle Fieldhouse in 1969. The Indianapolis school took the state title that year. McGinnis later starred for the Indiana Pacers in the ABA (at left) and in the NBA.

Heltonville's Damon Bailey (right), who became a standout at Indiana University, took a timeout for a photo in 1990, his senior year at Bedford-North Lawrence. He led the school to the state championship a month later.

Photo by Rich Miller

Reggie Miller joined the Indiana Pacers in 1987 after a stellar career at UCLA, where he won the John Wooden Most Valuable Player Award for three years. He's shown here in 1990 after being named an NBA All-Star.

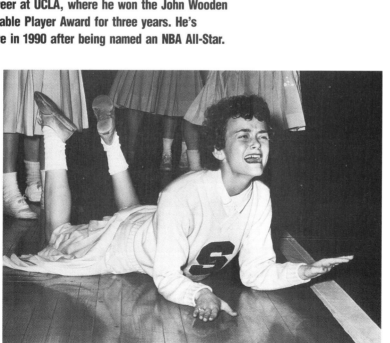

Losing can be so painful! Sharon Bruce, a cheerleader for Shortridge High School, pounded the hardwood after the Blue Devils lost a heartbreaker to Tech High School, 58-57, in the final seconds of their sectional matchup in 1961.

Photo by Joe Young

120

Reggie Miller's three-pointer with 5.9 seconds left stunned the Madison Square Garden crowd and sent the Indiana Pacers into overtime against the New York Knicks in 1998's Eastern Conference semifinals. The Pacers won, 118-107, to take a 3-1 lead in the series. They went on to win the series 4-1 but lost to Chicago in seven games in the Eastern Conference finals.

Photo by Paul Sancya

During the 1954 high school boys basketball tourney, members of the team from tiny Milan posed in a driver education car. Milan won the state title that year in the most memorable final game in the state's history. Bobby Plump, who scored the winning shot against Muncie Central in Butler Fieldhouse, is in the driver's seat. His teammates are (left to right) Ron Truitt, Ken Wendleman, Ray Craft, Roger Shroder and Gene White.

Photo by Frank Fisse

Before 1954's historic final game, there were the Pierceville Alleycats, who honed their skills at Pierceville near Milan: (from left) Glen Butte, Roger Shroder, legend-in-the-making Bobby Plump and Gene White.

Photo by Bob Doeppers

Indianapolis Star photo

As Milan's team prepared to travel to Indianapolis to take on Muncie Central for the state title, the town wore its heart on its store windows. The school was the smallest to make it to the finals since 1915.

The last-second shot by Bobby Plump drops through the net (below) to give Milan the 1954 state championship, 75-74, in its David-and-Goliath battle against Muncie Central. Plump is not visible.

Photo by James Ramsey

The day after Milan won the state championship, the Ripley County town of about 1,150 was joined by an estimated 40,000 visitors to watch the victory parade (left). The motorcade celebrating the title began with five cars in Indianapolis and was more than 13 miles long by the time it reached Milan.

Photo by William Palmer

123

Photo by Frank Fisse

Scenes for *Hoosiers* were being filmed in the St. Philip Neri gym in Indianapolis on Nov. 30, 1985 (above). The tale of underdogs at a tiny high school who won Indiana's state basketball championship was based on Milan's march to the title in 1954. The movie, starring Gene Hackman and Dennis Hopper, premiered in Indianapolis on Nov. 10, 1986.

The pride of Springs Valley High, Larry Bird, soars in the 1974 High School All-Star Game against Kentucky at Hinkle Fieldhouse (left). Bird averaged 22.9 points a game in 49 games in high school. He led Indiana State to the 1979 NCAA championship game, losing to Michigan State and Earvin "Magic" Johnson.

Photo by Jerry Clark

124

Photos by Mike Fender

On the day in 1995 when Seeger High's Stephanie White (above) became the all-time leading scorer in Indiana girls basketball, the line outside Fountain Central, where the game was played, was a half-mile long. White, whose Purdue team would win the national title in 1999, took care of her hair before game time.

Photo by Bob Doeppers

Indianapolis Star photo

Goalie Jimmy Franks (left) and center Don Deacon were star skaters for the Indianapolis Capitals of the International-American Hockey League in November 1939, when the team played at the Coliseum. The Capitals preceded the Racers, Checkers and Ice.

Seventeen-year-old Wayne Gretzky's journey to greatness passed briefly through Indianapolis. In 1978, Gretzky (above) signed a seven-year, $1.75 million personal services contract with Nelson Skalbania, who owned the Indianapolis Racers of the World Hockey Association. Gretzky played his first eight pro games in the city before moving on to Edmonton.

It was only the first period of the game against Fort Wayne, but Frank Bialowas of the Indianapolis Ice had already made an impact — on Dion Darling's face (right). The teams battled at Market Square Arena on March 6, 1999.

Photo by Matt Kryger

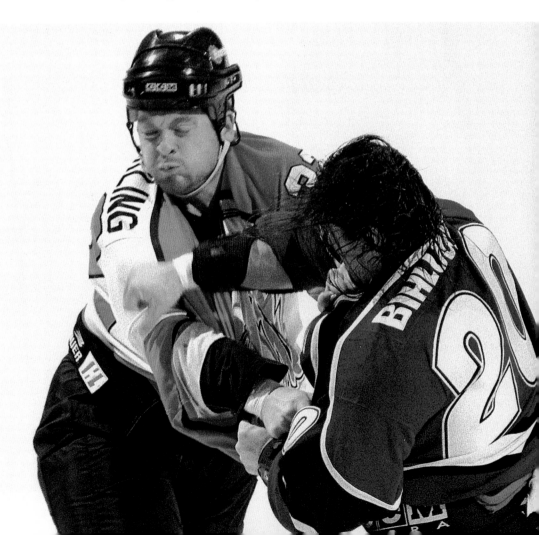

126

Photo by John Gentry

Runners and watchers fill a Downtown Indianapolis street with shadows in the 1993 500 Festival Mini-Marathon. The first mini-marathon in 1977 attracted 700 runners; 22,000 people took part in 1999.

Photo by D. Todd Moore

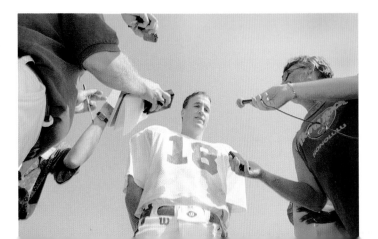

Indianapolis Colt Kerry Cash (above) lost his helmet in a hit from Cincinnati Bengal Darryl Williams at Riverfront Stadium on Sept. 12, 1993. There was no flag on the play. The Colts pulled out an ugly win, 9-6. Rookie quarterback Peyton Manning got a media workout after his first practice at the Colts' training camp in 1998 (left). Indianapolis made the University of Tennessee All-American its first draft choice.

Photo by Rich Miller

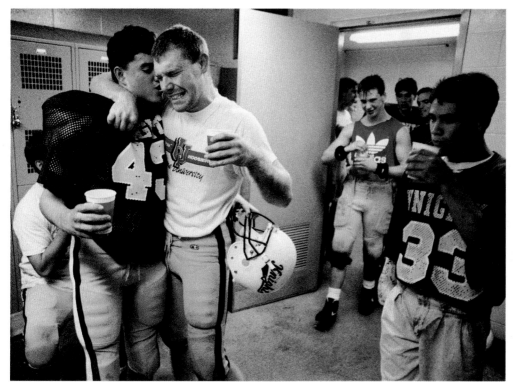

Knute Rockne (above), the University of Notre Dame's legendary football coach, compiled a 105-12-5 record from 1918 to 1931, fielding five undefeated teams. Rockne died in a plane crash in 1931; he was 42. Gridiron superiority was a new experience for Northeastern High School seniors Corey Anderson (left) and Jason Moore, who celebrated the school's first victory in five years after beating Cambridge City, 22-17, on Oct. 5, 1990. The Fountain City school had lost 46 straight.

129

Kathy Feldman (above) of Indianapolis tried to grab a souvenir from Paul Dawley, a batboy for the Indianapolis Indians, during a game against Iowa on April 14, 1992, at Bush Stadium.

At Market Square Arena, Greenfield's Jaycie Phelps (right), a member of the gold-medal-winning U.S. gymnastics team that became known as the Magnificent Seven of the 1996 Olympic Games at Atlanta, warmed up on the uneven bars (right) before a post-Olympics show.

The Downtown skyline competed with the base lines for spectators' attention during the Indianapolis Indians' first game at Victory Field (facing page), which opened on July 11, 1996. The stadium seats 13,250.

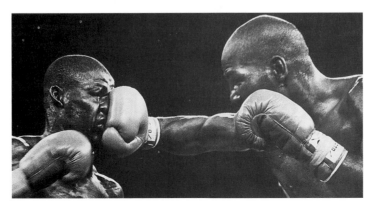

Marvin Johnson of Indianapolis lands a right to his opponent's nose during the successful defense of his light heavyweight title (left). Johnson won World Boxing Association titles in 1978, 1979 and 1985.

A late sprint pulled Kyrsten Abramson (above right), Meegan Amen and their teammates into second place in the Women's Eight division at the 11th National Rowing Championships. They represented a Seattle club at Eagle Creek Reservoir in 1987.

Indiana University swimming phenomenon Mark Spitz (right) brought home an unprecedented seven gold medals from the 1972 Olympic Games in Munich, West Germany. This photograph was taken in October of that year.

Photo by Jim Young

Photo by David Eulitt

Photo by Charlie Nye

Bodybuilder Peter Lupus, 21, is congratulated by Mr. Indiana of 1953, Earl Clark of Evansville, after being judged Mr. Indianapolis of 1954 (right). Lupus later built an acting career, becoming part of the cast of the television series *Mission: Impossible* from 1966 to 1973.

Photo by James C. Ramsey

Florence Griffith Joyner blazed across the finish line at the Indiana University Track Stadium at IUPUI on July 16, 1988, setting a world record in the 100-meter sprint at the Olympic Trials (above). Later that year, she won three Olympic golds at Seoul, South Korea. "FloJo" died of a seizure in 1998 at age 38.

Photo by Matt Kryger

Indianapolis Indians infielder Pete Rose Jr. had time to work on his bubble-blowing during fielding practice at Victory Field on April 8, 1998, the day before the Indians opened the regular season.

Photo by Charlie Nye

All eyes were on the ball as the United States' Insook Bhushan defeated Canada's Mariann Domonkos for a table tennis title at the Carmel Racquet Club during the 1987 Pan American Games.

A track meet in 1926 attracted large crowds to Arsenal Technical High School. Officially opened in 1916 as a manual and technical training school, it expanded its curriculum during the 1920s and, by 1930, had 242 teachers and 6,000 students.

Indianapolis News photo

Photo by Jim Young

Six riders landed hard during the 1988 Little 500 bicycle race at Indiana University's Bill Armstrong Stadium in Bloomington (above). The annual race became famous after the movie *Breaking Away*, based on the Little 500, came out in 1979. In Indianapolis, cyclists — including the one at right in 1993 — satisfy their need for speed at Major Taylor Velodrome. The track is named for Marshall "Major" Taylor, a black cyclist from Indianapolis who was America's top rider at the turn of the century.

Photo by Rob Goebel

135

Ray Harroun won the first 500-Mile Race at the Indianapolis Motor Speedway in a Marmon Wasp on Memorial Day 1911. After starting 28th, Harroun led 88 of the 200 laps in the only one-man car in the field.

Auto Racing

On May 30, 1911, men in four-wheeled racers negotiated the 2.5-mile Indianapolis Motor Speedway oval in the first 500-Mile Race. Ray Harroun, averaging 74.60 mph, took the checkered flag after a 6-hour, 42-minute contest. No one imagined the mantle of prestige this race would take on, or the international fame bestowed upon the brave souls who endured hour upon hour of grueling competition to capture the most coveted prize in auto racing.

For most of the next 83 years, the Brickyard, as the Speedway affectionately is known, was home to one race a year — the Indy 500. But with the raging popularity of stock car racing in the 1990s, a second annual race was inaugurated. Beginning in 1994, NASCAR's "good ol' boys" came storming onto the scene early each August for the Brickyard 400. The race captured the hearts of fans so quickly that it has became just as big an event as the Indy 500.

Big-time racing hasn't been limited to Indiana's oval tracks — drag racers have been pairing off in the NHRA U.S. Nationals at Indianapolis Raceway Park in eastern Hendricks County since 1961.

For the fans who come from far and wide, it just doesn't get any better than racing Indiana-style.

Victory in the first NASCAR Brickyard 400, run at the Speedway on Aug. 6, 1994, went to former Hoosier Jeff Gordon. The 23-year-old driver who took the racing circuit by storm lived at Pittsboro, in neighboring Hendricks County, from 1984 to 1991.

A crash in the front straightaway at the start of the 1973 race left Salt Walther severely burned, legs protruding from the car. Driver Wally Dallenbach is in the foreground. Eleven spectators were injured. Walther recovered to race again.

Photo by Jim Young

Ron Dudley of Tulsa, Okla., escaped with minor burns after his funny car caught fire during the National Hot Rod Association's U.S. Nationals at Indianapolis Raceway Park on Sept. 3, 1987 (above). A fire in 1941 destroyed the south garages at the Speedway — and three cars — four hours before the race.

Indianapolis Star photo

138

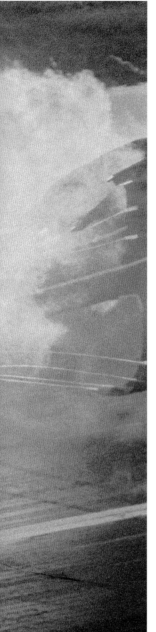

Photo by Vern Atkins

Photo by George Tilford

Lawrence Bisceglia, a 60-year-old semiretired auto mechanic from Long Beach, Calif., and his companion, Wiggles, made themselves at home outside the Speedway on April 3, 1958, the ninth straight year that he was first in line for the 500. Bisceglia was first for 38 years; his last race was in 1987.

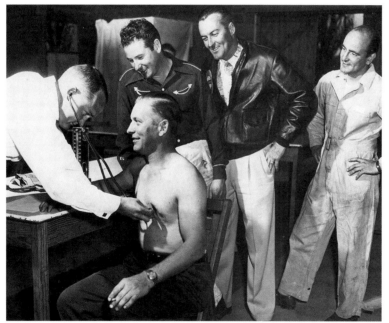

Photo by George Tilford

Getting his checkup from Dr. William M. Kelley of the Speedway medical staff on May 14, 1952, was Tony Bettenhausen; the kibitzers waiting their turn were (from left) drivers Rodger Ward, Johnnie Parsons and Manuel Ayulo. Ward would win the race in 1959 and 1962; Parsons took the checkered flag in 1950.

The gates of the Speedway opened 15 minutes late on the first day of qualifications on May 18, 1957, and the result was traffic jams for miles on West 16th Street (left) and all the other surrounding streets. Practice was delayed 45 minutes to permit a crossing to the infield over the main stretch of the track.

Photo by William Palmer

These spectators in 1950 (above) were just a few of the fans who've made the month of May unlike any other. In 1994, autographs were a priority (near right) at the first Brickyard 400. The 500 has been a tradition for CBS *Late Show* host David Letterman (middle right), seen yukking it up at the track in '93. He's been a fan since his youth in the Circle City. Enjoying a few drinks is another 500 tradition (far right).

Photo by Rich Miller

Photo by Steve Smith

Photo by Patty Espich

Indianapolis Star photo

141

Forty-three drivers thunder away on the first lap of the first Brickyard 400. The excitement of the start was matched by the finish, when Jeff Gordon fended off challengers to win by 53 hundredths of a second.

Charles Merz's Stutz races past the judges' pagoda in the 1912 Indianapolis 500 (near right). He finished fourth. Joe Dawson won that year, averaging 78.71 mph. The 1992 race became famous for the closest finish ever (far right): Al Unser Jr.'s margin of victory over Scott Goodyear was 43 thousandths of a second.

In the 1930s, as in the years that followed, the infield of the Indianapolis Motor Speedway was a place for fans to see and be seen. In 1999, work was under way on the infield section of a road course for the inaugural U.S. Grand Prix Formula One race in 2000.

Indianapolis Star Photo

Photo by Mike Fender

Photo by Paul Sancya

Photo by Mike Fender

Four unforgettable Speedway figures: Jeff Gordon, who kissed the track's bricks after winning the 1998 Brickyard 400 (above left); A.J. Foyt and his four winning cars, on May 22, 1987 (above); and Tony Hulman and his wife, Mary Fendrich Hulman, at the track in 1949 (left). The Hulmans bought the deteriorating Speedway for $750,000 in 1945 and turned it into the world's premier motorsports showcase. Hulman died in 1977, his wife in '98.

Photo by Dale Schofner

A pall descended on the Speedway soon after the
start of the 1964 race. Dave MacDonald's car hit the
fourth-turn wall and exploded; Eddie Sachs' car exploded after hitting MacDonald's. Both drivers died.

Parnelli Jones takes the fastest way out of a car fire
on the 55th lap of the 1964 race. He had steered the
Agajanian-Bowes car into the retaining wall after it

caught fire while entering the pits. Jones' premature
finish was sandwiched between his best performances
at Indy, a win in 1963 and second place in 1965.

Painters work on the scoreboard behind the pits prior
to qualifications in 1929. The American Automobile
Association decreed there should be only one car for
every 400 feet of track, limiting the field to 33.

148

Bill Cheesbourg celebrated with a cigar after his qualifying run in 1961 (top left). On race day, he got tangled up in a crash and finished in the 28th position. Cheesbourg competed six times at the Speedway from the late '50s to the mid-'60s. For television talk show host Johnny Carson, the fit of the STP Turbocar was a bit snug during the shooting of a segment for *The Tonight Show* in 1967 (middle left). In 1989, future Brickyard 400 champ Jeff Gordon (bottom left) was a 17-year-old sprint car driver at the Winchester (Ind.) Speedway. "The fastest woman on wheels" after her 162-mph run at the Bonneville Salt Flats, Paula Murphy (top right) took a tour of the Speedway in the famed Novi in 1963. In 1991, Willy T. Ribbs (bottom right) became the first black driver to qualify for the 500. He made an early exit with engine failure. Ribbs had better luck in 1993, completing 194 of the 200 laps.

Photo by Charles A. Berry

Love was in the air — along with the peace signs — on July 15, 1968, when an Indianapolis park provided an appropriately free-form setting for a wedding (above). Attire was strictly casual.

Residents of the Marion County Children's Guardian Home set the stage for a photo published in *The Star* the Sunday before Thanksgiving in 1959 (facing page). The home provides a haven for youngsters whose parents, for a variety of reasons, can't care for them. Some stay just a few hours, some a few months.

Photo by James Ramsey

Variety of Life

Solomon wrote in the book of Ecclesiastes, "There is a time for every event under heaven — a time to give birth, and a time to die; a time to plant, and a time to uproot what is planted, a time to kill, and a time to heal; a time to tear down, and a time to build up. A time to weep, and a time to laugh; a time to mourn, and a time to dance." It is that way today, just as it has been throughout the ages. The variety of life has many expressions. Offsetting painful times and difficulties are happy times when all seems right. Moments of pleasure and playful respite have always made the hard times more bearable. During the joyful times of life, the human spirit is lifted and blessed. Cares seem distant, replaced with cheerfulness and frivolity. This can be seen in the exuberance of youth, in the richness of camaraderie: close friends out for an evening on the town, children playing in their back yards, adults reliving the good times of their youth. Human behavior is hard to anticipate. We may be creatures of habit, but our God-given ability to adapt to our surroundings makes for some fascinating moments. Some people have used creativity as an outlet for expression of their individuality, in work and in recreation. For others, interesting moments arise out of the unpredictability of what life brings their way. Hoosiers always have been unbridled by the limits of human imagination. Each person leaves a unique imprint on life.

Photo by William Palmer

Photo by Rich Miller

More than 2,600 people attended the convocation and reunion banquet (top) to initiate 828 men into the Indianapolis Scottish Rite on April 10, 1965, at the Scottish Rite Cathedral, the world's largest.

Couples filled the Indiana Convention Center on April 15, 1985, for the "early bird qualifier" square dance (above). The event was for those who had registered early for the National Square Dance Convention.

152

Photo by Frank Fisse

An *Indianapolis Star* series published in 1953 found that slum or substandard housing was a problem in nearly 20 percent of Indianapolis. This area, in the 1200 block of Senate Avenue, eventually was razed.

In 1948, overseeing the records room in the Marion County Courthouse (above) was R.H. Shinkle's job. The building (left) was razed in 1962 and replaced by the City-County Building. Demolition of the courthouse began in June, with the southeast corner falling to wrecking crews.

The razing went much faster on Nov. 5, 1989, when the eight-story Occidental Building came down in 7.5 seconds (facing page). The structure at Illinois and Washington streets was leveled by 361 explosive charges to make way for Circle Centre.

Photos by Patty Espich

The corner of 19th Street and College Avenue was known for prostitution and other criminal activity in 1967. "The College Room" at 1812 College Ave. was opened in July of that year to provide young people with a safe place to hang out. Meeting at the chess board there were (from left) Paul Jones, Joe Crow and Manuel Robinson.

Photo by George Tilford

Katia Berezina waits backstage at Park Tudor School, where her Soviet ballet company gave two performances on Feb. 18, 1987, during a U.S. tour. At 13, Katia was the youngest of the teen-age dancers from Perm State Choreographic School, 600 miles east of Moscow.

Photo by Mike Fender

Photo by Tim Halcomb

Bowling's not that easy to begin with; and when you begin with a ball that's an armful, it's even harder. But Penny Endicott (above) was undeterred. The 4-year-old stayed focused on the game in April 1971.

Photo by Patty Espich

A trio of trash cans came in handy for hide-and-seek in the Heather Hills addition in 1967 — that is, until 5-year-old Mary Kay Stewart lifted the lids (above). At that moment, the game was up for Doug Penley (center), his brother Greg (left) and Andy Szabo.

When the Hula Hoop craze hit Indianapolis in 1958, stores found it difficult to keep up with demand. One enthusiast was 17-year-old Lillian Della-Penna, who demonstrated her technique on Sept. 7.

Photo by Joe Young

In March 1914, *The Gambler's Oath* was playing at My Theatre at Udell and Clifton streets in Indianapolis. The theater "gathers in the nickels," a story said.

Pennies counted for milk drinkers in February 1953, when the price was cut by 1 cent a bottle. To illustrate, milkman Walter Tierney (right) lined up 12 bottles at a home in the 4300 block of Park Avenue: Customers would get a free pint in the cost of 12 quarts.

You don't have to be driving a four-wheeler to use the drive-through at Orange County Bank in Paoli; a four-footer will do just as well. An Amish woman's ride, and a companion inside, waited up ahead as she took care of business in January 1998.

Photo by Kelly Wilkinson

Max Adams, director of 1952's third annual Indianapolis Custom Auto Show, mans the cockpit of a Jetmobile (below). The creation of Boonsboro, Md., draftsman Richard Harp was made from three aircraft-surplus gas tanks — a belly tank and two wingtip auxiliary tanks — and was capable of reaching 110 mph.

Photo by Maurice G. Burnett

A Wright Flyer biplane made a low pass during a local air show around 1910. The aviation shows were popular at sites throughout the Indianapolis area, including the Indianapolis Motor Speedway.

"Fly me to the moon," the old song goes; but the
moon was about 239,000 miles away. A much closer
landing spot was Indianapolis International, where
this airliner was headed on the night of July 19, 1997.

"Little people" caught the attention of the crowd when the Ringling Bros. and Barnum & Bailey Circus pitched its tents for a one-day show near the Indianapolis Motor Speedway in August 1950. Garnering the lion's share of publicity was a female gorilla called Mrs. Gargantua, who traveled in air-conditioned quarters.

When the Gentry Brothers Dog and Pony Show stopped in Indianapolis on May 10, 1933, 11-year-old Louise McNutt (left) got to go backstage to meet the performers. Louise's father, Paul McNutt, served as governor of Indiana from 1933 to 1937.

Indianapolis Star photo

"Dinah," the skeleton of a giant ground sloth at The Children's Museum, presented quite a sight for visitors on Jan. 13, 1952. The world's fourth-oldest children's museum opened in Indianapolis in 1925.

The Young Americans form an eight-person pyramid (above) at Circus City Center in Peru, Ind. The only group to perform the high-wire act, it won an international competition in Monaco in January 1999. Six months later, spiritual heights were reached at the Billy Graham Crusade in the RCA Dome (right).

Photos by Kelly Wilkinson

Photo by Guy Reynolds

The faces of the Indianapolis Children's Choir are reflected in a grand piano during a rehearsal for holiday performances. The two concerts at Second Presbyterian Church in December 1995 were sold out. The choir has been a hit outside the city as well, visiting countries from Norway to New Zealand.

The 47th annual National Day of Prayer on May 7, 1998, brought Paula Bollen, from Immanuel House of Prayer in Indianapolis, to the Indiana Statehouse to join others in supplication and song. Participants offered up prayers for federal and state leaders, families, police and teachers, among others.

Photo by Kelly Wilkinson

The popularity of TV was soaring in 1952, when election returns drew a crowd at the Indianapolis home of Robert Roesener (above). The Roeseners (at right) were joined by Mr. and Mrs. Henry Bettge (left) and Harold Kohlmeyer. In front were Stephen Bettge (left) and Steve and Fred Roesener.

The were plenty of screens to go around in late 1994 at the Sega/Nintendo Arena, which received the full attention of customers at Totally Kids day-care center near Castleton Square Mall on the Far Northside.

Mock rescues were among the activities at Warren Township's "Firefighter for a Day" camp, where 7-year-old Jacob Grass had his hands full on July 7, 1999. The camp was designed to let kids do what firefighters do for a few hours, including washing the trucks. Fire safety lessons also were provided.

Photo by Patty Espich

"Christmas can come to this little girl. Those great big dolls now are near but yet so far from the arms of this needy child," the caption for this *Indianapolis Star* photograph declared in December 1951. The picture accompanied an appeal to readers for contributions to the newspaper's Santa Claus Fund.

Photo by Maurice G. Burnett

167

Wiley B. Embry (left) was an umpire in the minor leagues, a truck driver and a dockworker. In 1984, he became something else — a heart patient. The Southport resident's ordeal intensified in 1988 when, at the age of 44, he learned that he needed a transplant. Embry would have to wait more than two years for the transplant operation, which was performed at Indiana University Hospital (below). The heart that would save his life was carried to the operating room in a cooler (right). The surgery on Jan. 15, 1991, took seven hours. It was a success.

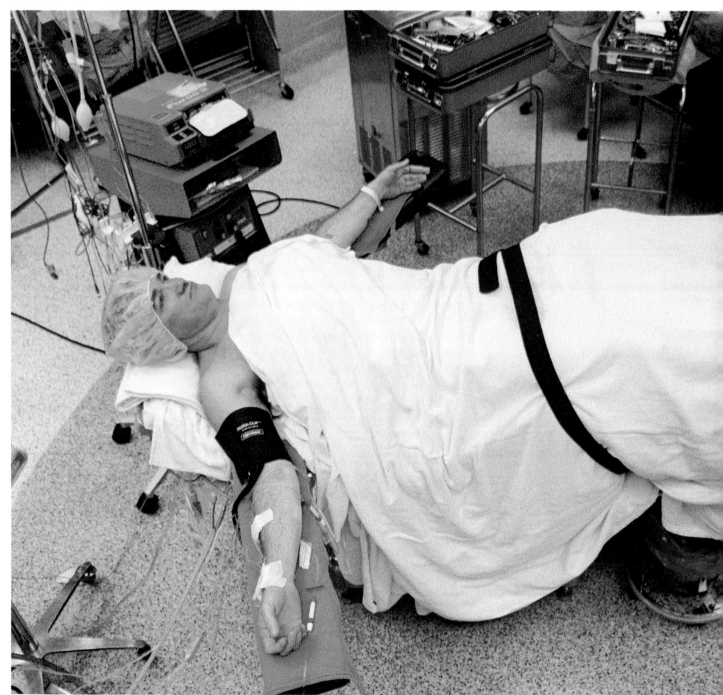

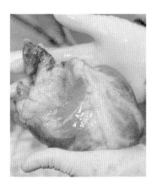

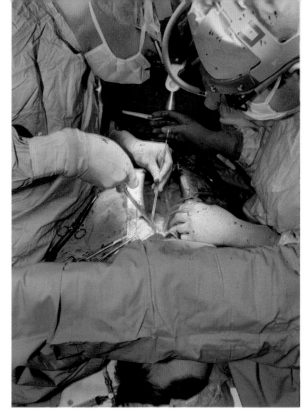

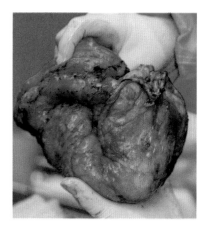

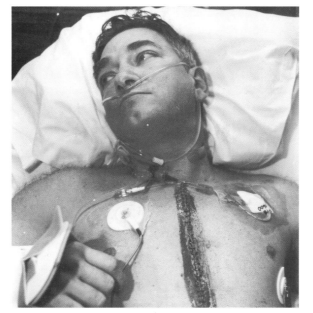

Embry's heart (above) was massively enlarged, while the donor heart (above far left) was about the size of a fist and had three times the pumping function of his heart. Three days after surgery (lower left), Embry's improved circulation made him feel more alert. Since cold air puts more stress on the heart, he wore a mask (below) to warm the air as he walked with his wife, Valentine. In September 1999, eight years after the transplant, Embry learned that his heart had come from an 18-year-old girl.

Photos by Jeff Atteberry

On an overheated day in June 1983 when the temperature in Indianapolis climbed to 90 degrees, 14-month-old Caitlin Murt (above) stayed comfortably and fashionably cool in the Jordan YMCA's pool.

Susan Percifield (left) of Vernon crosses the finish line at the Brown County Winter Festival bikini ski race at Nashville. The winner of the February 1981 event got to warm up in a $1,000 fur coat afterward.

Six-year-old Randall Ealy didn't let the absence of a lounge chair keep him from sunning himself on June 27, 1998. He simply improvised in front of his home in the 2800 block of Central Avenue in Indianapolis.

Scarves replaced bonnets on Easter Sunday 1964, when stiff winds and blowing snow forced Mr. and Mrs. Walter M. Mullen to abandon their effort to sell daffodils at 38th and Meridian streets (above). During a more appropriate month for such weather, an overnight fog covered the city of Indianapolis on Jan. 29, 1991, frosting the statue of Pan (left) and anything else that stood still long enough in Downtown's University Park.

Despite summer's heat, standing in line isn't as bad as it could be. Consumers waiting for a Paul Harris store to open for a back-to-school sale on Aug. 13, 1962, didn't appear to mind too much (right).

Lights in the sky echoed those below (facing page) after the lighting of the traditional Christmas "tree" on Monument Circle on Nov. 28, 1998. Lights first were strung on the Downtown landmark in 1962; now, thousands come to see the decorations switched on.

The $12 million Indianapolis Artsgarden (above), along with the adjacent Circle Centre mall, opened in September 1995. Owned by the Arts Council of Indianapolis, the glass-domed arts venue spans the intersection of Illinois and Washington streets.

Photo by James Ramsey

This toy Manchester weighed only 2.5 ounces when she was born on Nov. 19, 1952, at the George P. Lang kennels. It was the smallest the Langs had seen in 26 years of raising the breed. Here, she was a month old and weighed 8 ounces.

Dale, a dog of uncertain age and pedigree, enjoys climbing trees in pursuit of squirrels (below). He was spotted 12 to 15 feet up a tree in the Rocky Ripple area of Indianapolis on June 15, 1998. Dale learned to climb on his own, owner Jeff Chapman says.

Photo by Susan Plageman

Photo by Frank Fisse

Alfie, an Afghan hound, sometimes startled passers-by in 1972 when he'd pop up from behind a fence, looking like a neighborhood gossip. He was owned by Mr. and Mrs. James G. Stewart of Indianapolis.

Robert Sharp, Carl Middlebrook, Henry Green, Karl Brady and Edward Torrence (from left) baked 300 dozen Christmas cookies for hospital patients in Crispus Attucks High's food-handling class in 1960.

Union Station redcap Lang Wilson (above) was framed in steam from Amtrak's National Limited, the only passenger train serving Indianapolis, on Nov. 23, 1977. The station once served 100 trains and thousands of travelers daily.

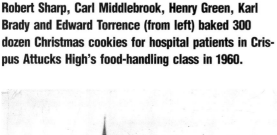

In Downtown's University Park, women celebrated the 10th anniversary of the Depew Memorial Fountain with interpretive dance in April 1926 (left). The figures in the center of the fountain represent the joys of dancing; the figure at the top represents the wonder of music.

175

The country line-dancing craze filled dance floors in Indianapolis as well as the rest of America. On Oct. 17, 1994, 21-year-old Jenni O'Brien was out in front in white hat and Western garb at Rawhide Western Dance Ranch, 3651 E. Raymond St. (above).

Break dancing went from New York to nationwide in 1983 after the movie *Flashdance* came out. By March 1984, these Indianapolis youngsters were polishing their moves near 41st Street and Rookwood Avenue.

Photo by Mike Fender

Dove Bohon (above) peers out from a high chair in the dining hall at Padanaram, the utopian communal village founded by nondenominational preacher Daniel Wright in 1966 in southwestern Indiana. The village, named for an Old Testament site, was home to more than 200 people in September 1989. To the north, Sandra lived as a patient at the Fort Wayne State School for the mentally handicapped (left). Designed for a maximum of 1,200 patients, the facility was struggling in 1964 to care for 2,250.

Photo by Ed Lacey Jr.

The Claypool Hotel (above) was built in 1903 at Washington and Illinois streets, on the site of the old Bates House, where President Abraham Lincoln addressed a crowd in 1861. Many political decisions were made in the hotel's smoke-filled rooms. It was razed in 1969; the site is now home to Claypool Court and the Embassy Suites. Another modern-day feature of Downtown is the horse-drawn carriage as entertainment; in 1918, this horse-drawn sleigh (below) was a necessity for these travelers.

A busy thoroughfare today, Illinois Street was bustling
around 1905, too. This view is looking south toward
Union Station from the Washington Street intersection;
the Claypool Hotel is at right in the foreground.

In 1906, Indianapolis' City Market (above) already was in its 20th year of operation. This view was shot from Alabama Street. In 1964, City Market supporters (left) packed a hearing room in a successful protest of health officials' threat to close the market.

Photo by Larry George

Traffic snarls have been a headache for a long time; witness this Sept. 29, 1950, morning rush hour on Washington Street in Downtown Indianapolis. The trackless trolleys (foreground) were discontinued in 1957.

The horses were giving their all in the effort to free this wagon from a rut at Kentucky Avenue and Henry Street in 1912, but it looked like they'd be needing some assistance.

181

A baby carriage served as a portable icebox (above) on Aug. 28, 1939, for a boy getting help from the Penny Ice Fund, which was conducted from 1931 to 1957 by *The Indianapolis Star* and the Salvation Army. The price of 1 cent for 25 pounds drew a line to Vermont and Koehne streets (below) on July 14, 1940.

In the Depression, some Indianapolis families were forced to live in tar-paper shacks (above) along Drover Street, on the west bank of White River. The area is now occupied by Truck and Bus Operations of General Motors Corp., Indianapolis Manufacturing Plant.

The newspapers published photographs of needy Hoosiers in 1950 (below) and 1951 (right) in appeals for donations to their charities, *The Star's* Santa Claus Fund and *The News'* Cheer Fund.

Photos by Maurice G. Burnett (below) and William Palmer (right)

Photo by Frank Fisse

Kids who petitioned Santa in 1956 (above) had wishes granted through the *The Star's* Santa Claus Fund. On Sept. 4, 1973, Kevin Huber likely wished to hang on to summer. School 54 teacher Carole Hon vetoed that.

Photo by William Palmer

184

The Indianapolis News' carriers gathered for an outing at Wonderland Amusement Park near Washington and Gray streets on the Eastside in 1908 (left). One popular attraction at the park, which opened in 1906, was a re-enactment of the 1889 Johnstown Flood in Pennsylvania that killed 2,200 people. The park burned down in 1911.

Photo by Charles Bretzman for The Indianapolis News

Departing with a sampling from the Marion County Library's Haughville branch in April 1952 were (left to right) Patrician and Fife Orebaugh and Purlene and Rose Marie Rogers. The branch's building, at 525 N. Belleview Place from 1901 to 1972, doubled as Haughville Town Hall for many of those years.

Indianapolis News photo

Photo by Frank Fisse

Everybody was in step, including the dog, as the 28th Infantry Division staged the first public review of its wartime strength at Camp Atterbury on Jan. 27, 1951 (above). The 18,000 infantry and artillery men of Pennsylvania's famed Keystone Division had just completed 11 weeks of basic training. Another military engagement found Anthony Rains (second from left) leading an attack on his 22-month-old brother, Kyle, in the Rainses' front yard (right) in August 1987.

Photo by Rob Goebel

Photos by Tommy Wadelton

After a concert at Fort Wayne's Memorial Coliseum for 10,000 screaming teens and their awed parents in May 1957, Elvis Presley was quiet and courteous at a news conference (above). The King's farewell-tour show before entering the Army was his first performance in Indiana, and his fans were ready (right).

Photo by Frank Salzarulo

Photo by Joe Young

The Beatles — (clockwise from lower left) George Harrison, Ringo Starr, Paul McCartney and John Lennon — arrived Sept. 3, 1964, for a Coliseum concert. On Aug. 25, 1965, their movie *Help!* also drew crowds (above right), including poster-toting fans Lana Stephens (left) and Gloria Willett of Greenfield.

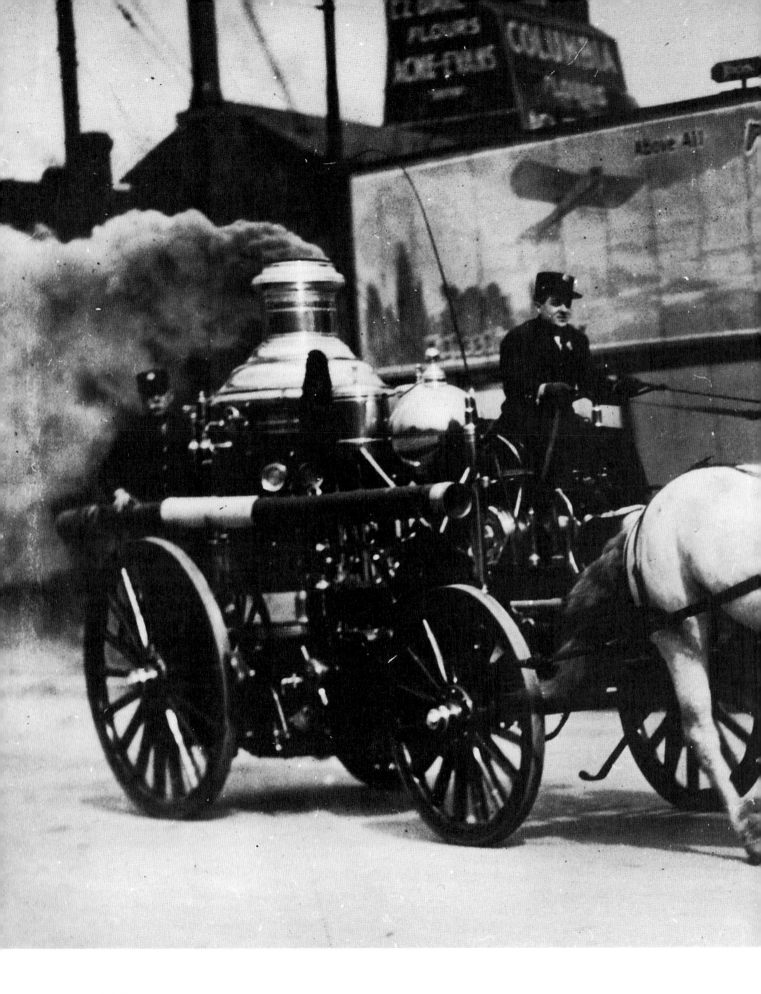

Firefighter Charles Gregory drove one of the Indianapolis Fire Department's Ahrens steam engines, housed at the old No. 6 station, on a simulated fire run down West Washington Street near Blackford Street in 1911. Riding in the back was engineer John Stake. The horses on duty that day were Bob (left), who liked onions, and Hoagy, who favored apples. The days of the horse and fire wagon soon would pass: In 1921, the department was completely motorized.

"What in science, art or sculpture
Has the merit to inspire
Greater human admiration
Than their dashes to a fire?
High above the engine's rumble
Sounds the driver's urgent shout,
And we thrill at every hoof-beat
When the Six's grays are out!"

Passage from *When the Six's Grays are Out*, a poem by William Herschell, which appeared in *The Indianapolis News* on April 22, 1911.

Indianapolis News photo

189

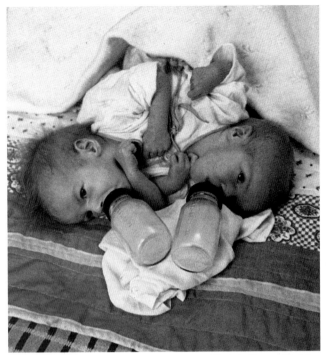

CHAPTER 9

Photo by Tommy Wadelton

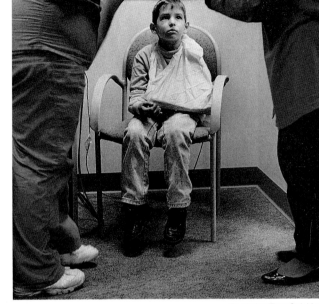

Photo by Tom Strickland

Daniel Kaye and Donald Ray Hartley (above left) drew worldwide attention when they were born joined at the waist on Dec. 11, 1953, in Washington, Ind. Their parents, Cecil and Margaret Hartley, already were raising three other young children in a home with no electricity or running water.

During its effort to record how health care was being conducted in one 24-hour period, *The Indianapolis News* photographed 6-year-old Cort Hawkins (above right), who broke his wrist when he fell off a swing at school. He could only sit and wait while his mom, Lisa Hawkins, talked with nurse Sue Inman.

Essays

W riters' stories are woven with carefully chosen words: descriptive adjectives, lively adverbs and graceful phrases. Likewise, photographers construct storytelling pictorials by capturing a variety of images that, when viewed as a whole, give viewers greater understanding. Striving for completeness, photographers often spend long periods of time with subjects, to the point where their presence goes almost unnoticed. Transcending superficial situations, a photographer's work can capture intimate, telling moments. The result of such intense pictorial scrutiny is a photo essay that, image upon image, weaves together an insightful look into people's lives. Probing beyond the obvious and venturing behind the scenes, photographers capture raw emotions played out in real time. These two essays, both health-related, depict the drama of life. The first story, from tiny Petersburg in early 1954, is a poignant look at coming to grips with the birth of conjoined twins. The pictures were taken over several months' time as a destitute family, tested to the utmost, faced a crisis. The second story is quite different, shot in just a 24-hour span by more than 30 photographers. "One Day of Health Care" is a look at the state of public and private health care on a typical day, Oct. 15, 1993. The documentary was in response to a national debate about health care in America.

The Hartley Twins

On Dec. 11, 1953, at Daviess County Hospital in Washington, Ind., an impoverished 28-year-old farm wife gave birth to twin boys who were joined at the waist but had two sets of shoulders and four arms.

The Hartley twins — Daniel Kaye and Donald Ray — instantly drew worldwide attention. Their parents, Cecil and Margaret, struggled to raise the twins and three other youngsters. Cecil traveled 50 miles a day from Petersburg to Crane Naval Depot, where he made $50 a week as a mechanic.

Star photographer Tommy Wadelton provided a glimpse at the hardships the family endured.

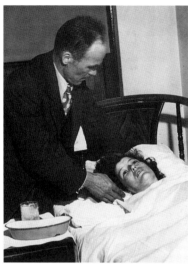

Photo by James Ramsey

Cecil Hartley talks with his wife, Margaret, in Daviess County Hospital the day after the twins were born. The babies spent their first 37 days at Riley Hospital for Children in Indianapolis. After a brief stint at home, they would return to Riley on March 18, 1954, after developing circulatory and breathing disorders. The problems abated for a short time, but more respiratory ailments led to their deaths on April 20, 1954. Residents of Petersburg (right) had kept up on the family's progress through the newspaper.

Photo by Tommy Wadelton

This tar-papered farmhouse near Petersburg in Pike County was the Hartleys' home when the twins were born. It didn't have electricity or indoor plumbing. After news of the birth spread, donations came in that allowed the family to move to a better-equipped home, which it rented for $30 a month.

Photo by James Ramsey

Cecil and Margaret Hartley pose with the twins at home. The couple had three other young children when the boys were born. Cecil worked at Crane Naval Depot, and gifts of help and money enabled the family to get by.

Photo by Tommy Wadelton

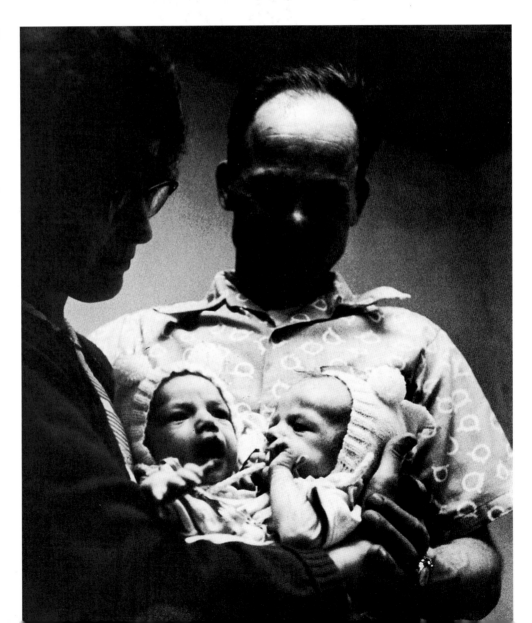

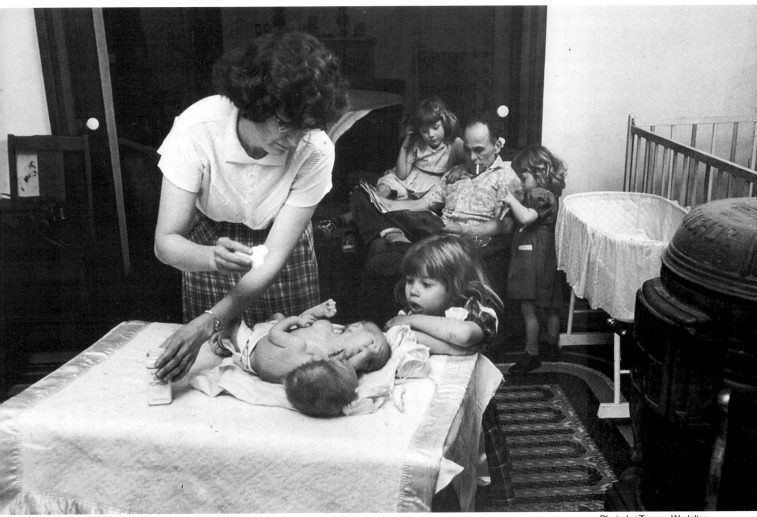

Two-year-old Shirley Ann pays close attention as her mother powders the twins during a diaper change. Mary Lou, 5½, and Connie Sue, 4, keep their father company while he does some reading.

A concerned and tired mom spends a moment with her 2-year-old daughter, Shirley Ann, as her twin sons undergo a medical examination (right) by Dr. Joseph W. Elbert, the family's physician. Elbert, of Petersburg, paid daily visits to the twins, who weighed 10 pounds, 7 ounces at birth.

Photos by Tommy Wadelton

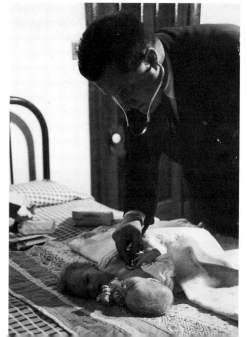

As her twins fought off respiratory ailments, life went on for Margaret Hartley. That meant tending to daily chores, such as hanging laundry out to dry (left) and shopping (below) at a Petersburg grocery store.

Photos by Tommy Wadelton

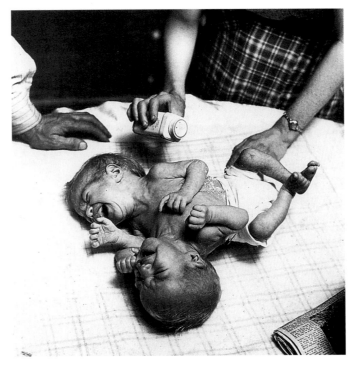

Baby powder appeared to have no soothing effect for Daniel Kaye and Donald Ray, voicing their displeasure after their diaper was changed (left). The boys died of respiratory problems in April 1954.

Photos by Tommy Wadelton

Margaret Hartley gets some advice (above) about legal and financial matters that cropped up after the twins were born. The couple also received hundreds of letters (right) as people around the world responded to the news about the family.

One Day of Health Care

In 1993, health care became one of the most talked-about issues in the nation. So *The Indianapolis News* launched a 24-hour project documenting how health care touches us from birth through death, sending 32 photographers and 19 reporters to dozens of health care sites in central Indiana on Friday, Oct. 15. After the team captured a vast array of images, the results were published a week later, Friday, Oct. 22.

In "One Day of Health Care," *The News* set out to personalize our country's sometimes frustrating, often miraculous system of medicine.

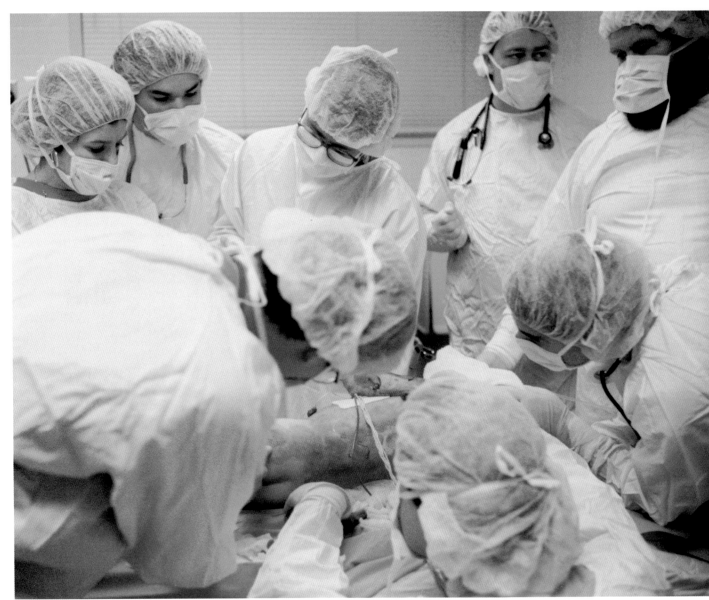

Photo by Rick Loomis

7:08 a.m. Wishard Memorial Hospital emergency room personnel assess the burns of the 3-year-old victim of a house fire. The child was flown to Wishard from Illinois and later was transferred to Riley Hospital for Children.

9:23 a.m.

Vials of insulin are labeled at an Eli Lilly and Co. factory in Indianapolis, home of the pharmaceutical giant. Lilly was the first company to bottle and sell insulin, which revolutionized treatment for diabetes.

10:45 a.m.

Louise Cox (left) greets Homeless Mobile Team nurse Debbie Rhodes with a kiss. Thanks to Rhodes and her team, an outreach project of Midtown Mental Health Center, the formerly homeless Cox was able to move to the Lugar Towers apartment building for senior citizens on limited incomes.

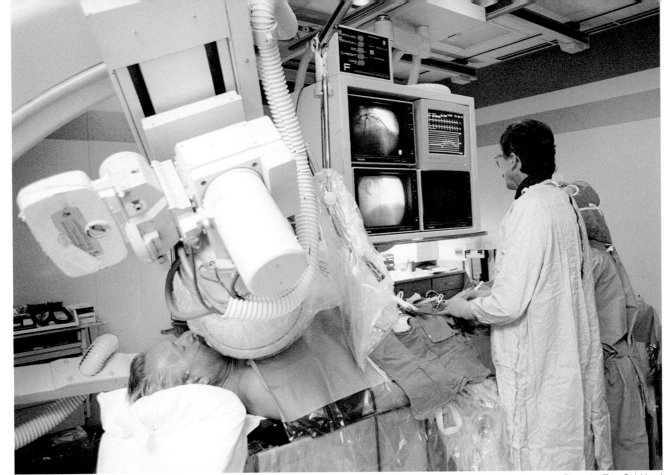

2:43 p.m.

At St. Vincent Hospital, Dr. Tom Linnemeier performs an angioplasty on 56-year-old Edward Kaiser of Peru. During the procedure, a tiny balloon is inserted into an artery to clear it.

2:45 p.m.

Rick, a 36-year-old AIDS patient at Community Hospital East, said he was a drug user who contracted the disease through contaminated needles. He had full-blown AIDS for two years and spent his time at the hospital. Rick, who called his intravenous machine "Jesus," said, "AIDS is the devil's disease. I'd never wish this on anybody." Rick died on Jan. 25, 1994.

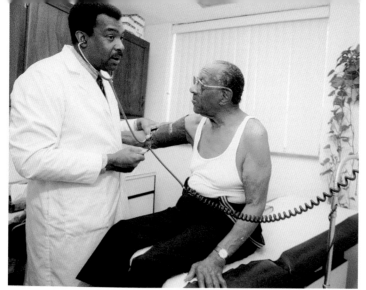

Photo by John Gentry

3:05 p.m.

Dr. Freeman Martin checks the blood pressure of Hillard Reed, a patient in his Northside geriatric practice. As the population of America ages, the cost of providing geriatric care is likely to increase dramatically.

6:41 p.m.

Dr. Edmund Gomez presents Garrett Jordan Goodbar to his parents, Cynthia and Bob Goodbar. The baby was one of nine born at Methodist Hospital on Oct. 15. Nurse Joyce Reynolds shared in the happy moment.

Photo by Rich Miller

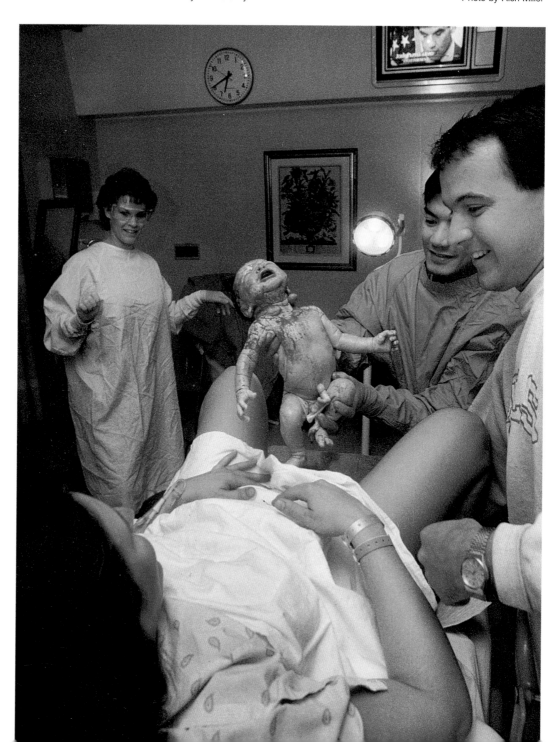

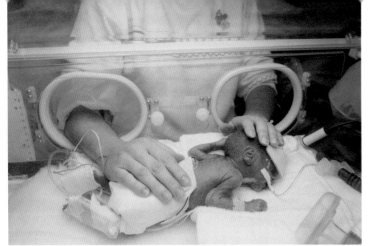

6:55 p.m.

Two-day-old Michael Lee Fouts sleeps under the blue lights of his isolette in Methodist Hospital's neonatal intensive care unit. The most medically expensive years of life are generally the first and the last.

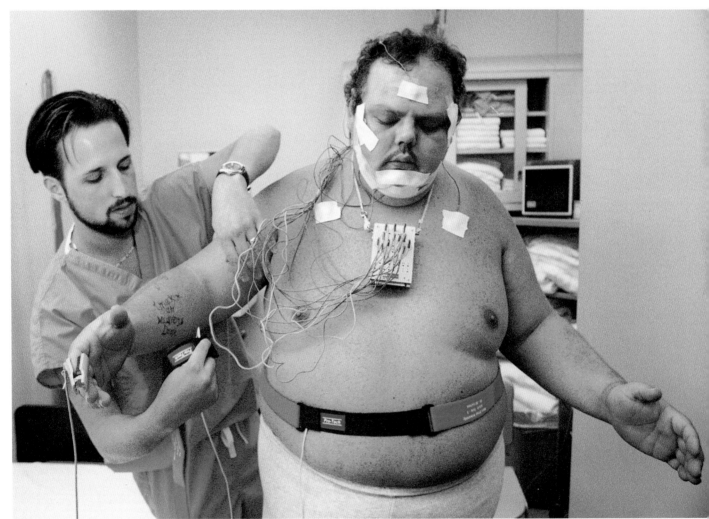

9:23 p.m.

Indiana University Hospital's sleep lab helps people determine what is preventing a good night's rest. But monitoring is an involved process, Johnny W. Baker Jr. learns as he's hooked up by Christopher Hummel.

Indianapolis News photo

Photographers used bulky cameras on tripods to record ceremonies marking the laying of the cornerstone of the Indiana World War Memorial on July 4, 1927. The color guard is facing north.

Changing Focus

Today's cameras are a far cry from the days of old. Early cameras were bulky and used glass plates upon which the images were fixed. The emulsions were very slow, requiring lengthy exposures, even in bright sunlight. As the photographic equipment improved, film speeds increased and cameras became more portable.

The dominant camera from the 1940s into the 1960s was the Speed Graphic. This camera used celluloid film instead of glass plates, but the camera still exposed pictures one at a time, requiring a film holder to be inserted in the back of the camera, then the exposure made. Most press photographers used 4-by-5-inch film.

Although color film was available, the extra time required to prepare color pictures for publication largely prohibited wide use. Even into the 1980s, the newspapers primarily printed photos in black and white.

In the 1960s, smaller, unobtrusive 35 mm cameras came into

Indianapolis News photo

Indianapolis News photographer George Tilford (left) hoisted a new Speed Graphic camera on June 3, 1956. Using celluloid film rather than glass plates, the Speed Graphic ruled in news photography from the '40s on into the '60s. Negatives were 4 inches by 5 inches.

Indianapolis Star photo

Indianapolis Star photographer William A. Oates (above) uses a Pentax camera with a 20-power eyepiece on a Bausch & Lomb telescope to photograph craters on the moon. An amateur astronomer, Oates took the photos in his back yard in August 1965.

wide use. They made it easier to take a large number of pictures, up to 36 on a roll of film. They proved so popular that the traditional Speed Graphics, synonymous with news photographers for so many years, began to be retired.

By the 1970s, motor-driven attachments allowed the cameras to take as many as three or four frames a second. This proved especially valuable in covering sporting events, which up to this point had proved to be a great challenge when shooting single-frame action. While more limiting, the Speed Graphics had forced photographers to have great discipline. Since film was relatively cheap, especially black and white film, photographers began exposing more pictures on assignments than their predecessors did with the bulkier cameras.

As film speeds increased, available-light photography gave photographers more freedom of movement (not having to carry around a big flash, or strobe light). It also gave a more natural look to the pictures. Backgrounds did not go completely black, as they did with flash

Photo by John Gentry

Photo by George Tilford

photography.

Photographers today sometimes use multiple flash on one exposure (especially useful in sports arenas), although the practice actually was more widespread in the 1950s. More often than not, today's shooters use fill flash (available light and strobe together) when shooting indoors or in brightly sunlit situations. This retains the natural lighting appearance in a scene, yet adds enough direct light with the flash unit to provide a good range of tones that will print well in the newspaper.

Today's 35 mm cameras offer an incredible range of interchangeable lenses. *The Star* owns lenses ranging from 14 mm to 600 mm. The lower the number, the wider the angle of view. The more powerful lenses are used mainly for sports and for spot news, when it's not possible to move in close to subjects. These lenses also make the backgrounds fuzzy — the reason that players in sports photos stand out so clearly from the crowds.

The biggest technological development in newspaper photography has been the elimination of darkrooms. No longer do photographers have to go into total darkness, roll their film onto reels and submerge them in tanks of chemicals in a process that has to be very exacting in terms of time and temperature. This change was a very welcome one for most newspaper photographers, who spent much time in darkrooms, first processing their film, then hand-developing prints. Chemical fumes were not healthy to breathe, and frequently the developer left unsightly stains on clothing when chemicals splashed from trays.

In 1994, the walls to the darkrooms at *The Star* and *The News* began to come down as the newspaper converted from making prints to the digital scanning of images onto Macintosh computers. When the film emerges from an automatically fed machine operated in room light, it

Photo by Rich Miller

Photo by Patty Espich

Technology has brought the photojournalist's tools to a new level with digital cameras, which capture images on reusable disks instead of film. Pictured is the back of a 1998 Kodak DCS 520 (far left) with a Canon EOS 1N body, showing the image of the *Star/News* building on a preview screen. The use of an Apple G3 Powerbook portable computer (shown at near left) eliminates the need for a darkroom. Images from a digital camera are downloaded into the computer for editing, then sent by modem back to the newspaper office.

is edited by the photographer and picture editors. Selected frames are scanned into the computer. These digital files have replaced print processing in trays of chemicals.

Today's photographers must have not only photographic skills, but a good grasp of computer skills as well. Over the past 10 years, camera companies began mass-marketing digital cameras designed for photojournalists. These cameras store visual information in a digital format on computer chips rather than exposing an image onto light-sensitive film. A few newspapers in the country have gone fully digital, equipping photographers exclusively with filmless cameras, but *The Star* is still in a transition phase.

The Star and *The News* bought two digital cameras in 1995 and 1996. Digital cameras primarily were used in the news bureaus in the surrounding counties and for remote transmission from sporting events. They save valuable time by eliminating film processing. Instead, a digital card is removed, inserted into a computer and downloaded.

A major advantage to digital cameras is the cost savings for film, but there are drawbacks. Technology has been slow in matching the quality of film cameras, but recent improvements have closed the gap greatly. The quality of the newest line of cameras is very good, and it is hard to tell the difference on the published page between images produced with film and digital cameras.

In 1999, camera prices dropped dramatically. The cost of a digital camera that was practical for newspaper photography before 1999 was $13,000 (about six times the cost of a traditional film camera). Equipping a staff of 18 to 20 photographers, each with two cameras, is expensive. As the year 2000 approached, camera manufacturers began cutting prices; one manufacturer slashed prices in half. The photography staff now has more than 10 digital cameras to supplement traditional film cameras but by the end of 2000, *The Indianapolis Star* expects to eliminate the use of film, converting its photo department to a fully digital operation.

The digital camera is the wave of the future.

Below is the list of photographers whose work is represented in this book. They include full-time or part-time photographers for *The Indianapolis Star* and *The Indianapolis News*, as well as contract or free-lance photographers who shot photographs for the newspapers. Following each name is their newspaper affiliation and years of service.

Key: *(S) The Indianapolis Star*
(N) The Indianapolis News
(SN) Star and News after photo staffs merged in 1995
(C) Contract photographer (includes free-lance, stringer)

Photo by Maurice G. Burnett

In 31 years at *The Star*, Joseph Craven photographed every president since Teddy Roosevelt. Craven retired in 1953.

Photo by Bill Clouse   Photo by Jim Young

Patty Haley Espich was hired by *The News* in January 1960 and retired from *The Star* and *The News* in October 1999. Tommy Wadelton, a *News* photographer in 1948, became the *Star Magazine* photographer two years later.

Office of Tibet photo by Larry Sandborn

Special assignments in 1999 for *Star/News* photographer Robert Scheer (left) included the Billy Graham Crusade in Indianapolis and the visit to Bloomington and the capital by Buddhist spiritual leader the Dalai Lama (right).

Photo by Guy Reynolds

Is Bessie trying to get in the last word in this book, or is she just one of those cows who can't resist mugging for a camera? You decide. All that's certain is that she and her friends were seeking some relief in a pond near Lebanon on Sept. 2, 1993.